Alexander Graham Bell

Alexander Graham Bell

INVENTOR AND VISIONARY

KENDALL HAVEN

FRANKLIN WATTS
A Division of Scholastic Inc.
New York Toronto London Auckland Sydney
Mexico City New Delhi Hong Kong
Danbury, Connecticut

Photographs © 2003: Corbis Images: 10 (Ric Erginbright), 95 (Wolfgang Kaehler), 36 (Bob Krist), 107 (Underwood & Underwood), 40, 57; Library of Congress: 2, 12, 14, 18, 20, 24, 27, 30, 32, 34, 42, 46, 53, 60, 68, 84, 94, 100, 108, 112, 114; National Geographic Image Collection/Bell Family: 54; North Wind Picture Archives: 76, 89, 98; Parks Canada/Alexander Graham Bell National Historic Site of Canada: 21, 88; Photo Researchers, NY: 71 (J-L Charmet/SPL), cover bottom right (Library of Congress/SPL), 74 (Mark Marten/Library of Congress), 79 (Sheila Terry/SPL), back cover ghost, cover top left, 6; Smithsonian Institution, Washington, DC: 92 (Charles Sumner Tainter Pictures, Archives Center, National Museum of American History).

Library of Congress Cataloging-in-Publication Data

Haven, Kendall F.

Alexander Graham Bell : inventor and visionary / by Kendall Haven.
  p. cm. — (Great life stories)

Summary: Explores the life of Alexander Graham Bell, the inventor of numerous devices, including the telephone. Includes bibliographical references and index.
ISBN 0-531-12314-6

1. Bell, Alexander Graham, 1847–1922—Juvenile literature. 2. Inventors—United States—Biography—Juvenile literature. [1. Bell, Alexander Graham, 1847–1922. 2. Inventors.]   I. Title.   II. Series.

TK6143.B4H38 2003
621.385'092—dc21

2003000960

Contents

Alexander Graham Bell demonstrates his most famous invention, the telephone.

Introduction

"**M**r. Watson, come here. I want to see you." Those simple words were the first ever spoken over a telephone. Alexander Graham Bell spoke them. He also invented the telephone over which they were spoken. In later years many claimed that the telephone was the one great achievement of the inventor's life.

Alexander Graham Bell did not agree.

Driven by unquenchable curiosity, Bell possessed an almost magical gift for seeing inventive possibilities and for envisioning how to create things that worked. He was driven by a deep need to solve problems and to invent practical solutions. No one invention ever satisfied Bell. There was always another problem to ponder, another invention to create.

Most people know that Bell invented the telephone, but few know that, within five years of its invention, Bell grew almost to hate the device and all it represented. Few know how close Bell came to losing the race to invent the telephone. Elisha Gray came within hours of beating him. Thomas Edison was hard at work on his own design.

Few know of Bell's work with the deaf. Yet that is how Bell thought of himself and how he thought he would be remembered. Even fewer think of Bell as a great visionary whose inventive ideas ran years ahead of his time. Bell drew a diagram for a working jet airplane in 1893. He invented the first metal detector and the first audiometer (a device to measure sound levels) as well as flat records, the stylus (or phonograph needles), and the unit of sound volume measure, the bel. He invented a precursor of fiber optics (now widely used in telecommunications networks) and developed much of our hydrofoil boat technology. Hydrofoils are underwater "wings" that allow ships to literally fly through water.

Alexander Graham Bell was the first to seriously consider resource shortages of fresh water and clean air, and he invented both water-recycling and water-recovery systems as well as water-desalination schemes.

Bell was an inventor, an extraordinary teacher of the deaf, a visionary, and a devoted family man. Bell was all of these and more. Bell grew up dreaming of a career as a concert musician. His music teacher agreed that he had a talent for it. But his father and grandfather helped to change the direction and focus of young Alexander's life and dreams. Alexander's career in speech and sound was their idea.

Alexander was born in Scotland. He lost both of his brothers to tuberculosis, a loss from which some think he never fully recovered. Alexander's father moved the remaining family to Canada to save Alexander from the same fate. By the time he was twenty-three, many of the things in his life that he had loved—his two brothers, the Scottish countryside, a life of music—had all been lost. Still, he succeeded. He excelled. Alexander Graham Bell became one of the brightest stars in the history of science and technological invention. In addition, Alexander Graham Bell makes for fascinating reading. This is his story.

The Birth of Invention

Alexander's earliest memory was of being taken over by a forceful curiosity about the natural world. It happened in Edinburgh, Scotland, on a brilliant summer afternoon in 1851 that was filled with warm sunshine, with none of the drizzle so common along the Scottish coast, and none of the coal-smoke haze that usually choked the bustling city. Professor Alexander Melville Bell packed his family into their carriage and drove to the countryside for a picnic. The family horse clomped over rough cobbles pulling Melville, his wife Eliza, and their three young sons past Queen Mary's Craigmillar Castle, past the craggy hill called Arthur's Seat, and out to the wide fields that spread toward the sea from Ferny Hill.

While Professor Bell and his wife spread blankets, young Melville (six), Alexander (four), and Edward (three) tumbled out to play. A wheat

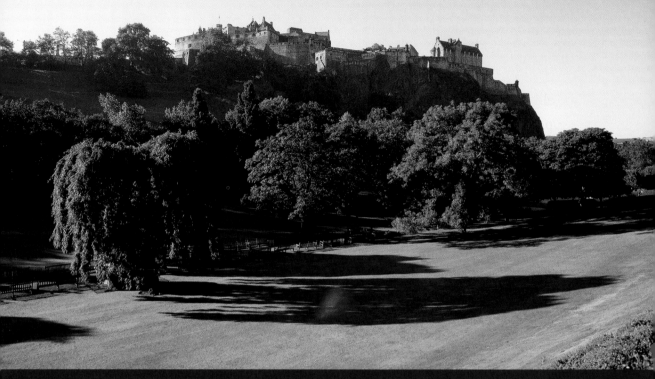

This photograph shows a park in Edinburgh. At the time Alexander was growing up, there were some places in the area where people could enjoy the beauty and wonder of nature.

Scotland's Industrial Revolution

Edinburgh was the first city in Scotland to experience the great industrial revolution of the mid-1800s. The profusion of steam engines and the development of steel and coal industries pushed individual craftspeople and cottage industries aside. They were replaced by factories that poured coal soot from countless chimney stacks. Everything, from fabrics to clothing, from steam trains to weapons, from shoes to pens, from plates to candlesticks, was suddenly produced faster and cheaper in giant factories.

field across the road drew Alexander's attention. Shimmering stalks of ripened grain swished against each other in the swirling wind and seemed to whisper to the boy.

Aleck (the name the family used for Alexander to avoid confusion since both his father and his grandfather were also named Alexander) was fascinated. He set off to explore, his mop of curly brown hair lost to sight in the sea of yellow grain. He had wondered if it was possible hear wheat grow. Hadn't he heard adults mention listening to the grain grow?

Aleck's brothers, his parents, and their picnic were forgotten. His mind filled with the sudden need to understand the sound of growth. He searched through the field for the voice of wheat. For a long time Aleck sat among the stalks, eyes clamped shut, straining to hear the sound and voice of growing wheat.

A large bird glided low overhead. The whisper of wind through its feathers caused Aleck to look up and to wonder in awe about the nature of sound itself—that magical thing everyone heard and yet no one could see.

Then Aleck realized that he was lost in the dense wheat. He couldn't see over the waving stalks to find his parents. The boy began to cry, but no one heard him. Nor did he hear the frantic shouts of his parents because he had cried himself to sleep in the field.

"Aleck! Aleck!" The deep tones of his father's voice awoke the boy and led him back to his mother's comforting arms. Years after the fright of being lost was forgotten, grown-up Alexander Graham Bell still remembered the excitement he felt while pondering the science questions he had thought about that afternoon.

Alexander's father, Professor Alexander Melville Bell, was well known for his work in elocution, or the art of public speaking. He pushed Alexander to be a better student.

A STUDENT OF *WHAT?*

Alexander was born on March 3, 1847, in Edinburgh, Scotland. He was named for his grandfather, who had performed as an actor in his youth and now taught elocution, or correct diction and speech, in London. The old man made a comfortable living treating stammering, lisps, and other speech defects.

Alexander's father, Professor Alexander Melville Bell, followed in his father's career choice, teaching elocution at the University of Edinburgh. He gained a worldwide reputation for his research and writings during Alexander's childhood years. Professor Bell's textbook, *The Standard Elocutionist*, sold more than 750,000 copies. By the time of his death, in 1905, he had written two dozen textbooks on speech that were used in universities and schools around the globe.

Alexander's older brother, Melville Bell, called Melly, seemed destined to follow their father's path. He excelled in every class. School and book learning came naturally to Melly. He enjoyed the process as if it were a game. Melly romped through his first years of formal schooling drawing consistent praise from his teachers.

Edward Bell, Alexander's younger brother by a year, also showed early promise as a conscientious and skilled student. Crammed in between the glowing reports on Melly and the early school successes of Ted (Edward's nickname), Aleck's work stuck out like a sore thumb. Aleck was described as an indifferent student. His school performance—or lack thereof—was a continual embarrassment to his father.

In truth, school bored Aleck. Studies, classroom recitations, and textbooks seemed a dreary and unending chore with little or no reward. Aleck loved to roam through the Scottish heather. Tramping over hills and meadows gave him a chance to wonder about the nature of oceans, of waves, or of birds' flight.

Education in Scotland

Education for children began at about age five, but at the time it was not compulsory. Only university students, nearly all boys, were schooled beyond the age of fourteen or fifteen. Some young children were taught at home by their mothers. Still, in 1850, many boys and most girls received very limited schooling. As young as eight and nine, most working-class children trudged to work in fields as agricultural laborers or marched into factories to work long hours at the new machines. Few hours of their day were reserved for attending school.

That was fine for a young boy learning to read and write from his mother. However, Professor Bell strongly disapproved of Aleck's lack of interest in serious schooling. Aleck's wanderlust would never do in formal schooling. It showed a lack of self-discipline. It wasted precious time needed for study. And Professor Bell wanted all three of his sons complete university study and follow him into teaching and scientific research.

Aleck's father was right in one sense. Aleck was a poor student, constantly criticized for not applying himself to his studies. Aleck longed to study zoology, nature, and natural sciences. He could see no practical value in learning Greek, Latin, physics, and literature, which were part of the college preparatory program his father insisted he take.

Alexander and Melly were quite the team growing up. This photograph shows the entire Bell family (left to right): Melville, Alexander Melville Bell, Edward, Eliza, and Aleck.

MISCHIEF'S THE THING!

The one place where Melly and Aleck saw eye to eye was mischief. They both had a natural gift for turning every moment into mischievous play.

When Aleck was eight, the boys' father mentioned needing to get his pocket watch cleaned. Aleck decided it was the perfect chance to do something nice for their father and to see how a watch worked. Aleck persuaded Melly to swipe the gold-backed watch from their father's dresser. Aleck quickly disassembled the watch, marveling at the precision and design of its tiny gears and springs as he spread its array of miniature parts across the kitchen floor. The boys washed each tiny piece with soap and water, and scrubbed them with a stiff fingernail brush. Aleck, amazingly, was able to reassemble the watch. It ran perfectly for two days before the specks of water they neglected to dry from individual pieces began to fog the watch's glass face and to corrode its innards.

The boys' mother praised their effort and ability. Professor Bell was neither impressed nor pleased.

In their off hours, the boys loved to play in a local grain mill owned by John Herdman, the father of a classmate of Aleck's. Once Herdman grew so tired of cleaning up after the boys and of repairing the chaos as they swirled through his mill that he dragged the boys into his office for a scolding. Aleck was ten, and Melly had just turned twelve.

Herdman's finger shook as he bellowed at them. Alexander later recalled that he ended by demanding, "Why don't you do something useful?" Herdman scooped up a handful of wheat. "Figure out how to remove the husks from this wheat. Now that would be useful!"

Aleck was delighted by the challenge. He soon discovered that they could scrape off the husks with a small nailbrush. Melly complained that "it required far too much work to make for good mischief."

The brothers agreed that they needed to think on a grander scale. Behind the mill Melly found an old vat with a rotating paddle wheel inside. Aleck attached rough, short-bristled brushes to the paddles. The boys eagerly poured grain into the vat and cranked a large handle to spin the paddles. Wheat berries slammed, scraped, and tumbled across the brushes. Thick dust rose to choke the boys and make their eyes water. But the wheat berries had been separated from their husks!

Herdman was so impressed that he built a second vat, following Aleck's design, and had both mounted on the wooden delivery dock of his mill. Even Professor Bell agreed that their invention was clever and useful. He also grumbled that the boys were wasting valuable time that should have gone to academic study. A half-century later, and through three owners, Aleck's wheat separator was still in use at the mill.

For days, Aleck carried a small bag of wheat in his pocket, sifting the separated grain through his fingers, marveling that his invention worked better than had the methods used by experienced adults. Using mechanical invention to solve problems was instantly ingrained as the hub of Bell's lifelong approach to work.

Inspired by his wheat-separator success, a newborn spirit of invention was kindled in Aleck's heart. As he passed through his teenage years, that drive to explore the world through invention brightened into a blazing comet that would never be quenched.

Family Forces

The piano at the Bell house sat in a back parlor, turned so that window light flooded across the keyboard. Of the three Bell boys, Aleck was the one naturally gifted musician. His mother, Eliza Bell, arranged for him to study with Auguste Benoit Bertini when Aleck turned ten. The renowned pianist felt that Aleck showed promise of a fine career as a concert pianist.

Ten-year-old Aleck sat on the piano bench, his fingers roaming across the ivory keys. His mother sat beside him. Though nearly deaf, she was a gifted pianist and passed her love of music on to Aleck. Often she held a rubber listening tube against the piano's soundboard to hear the notes he played. Sometimes she laid her hands softly on top of his and, eyes closed, seemed to hear the music by feeling the movement of his fingers.

When his mother raised a finger to comment, Aleck did not reply by speaking into her hearing tube. Aleck had learned that she could understand his words if he spoke in low, steady tones right against her forehead. Others said it was a waste of time and shouted into her tube. But Aleck and his mother shared a uniquely close bond. Aleck alone had the patience to speak to his mother without mechanical aid.

Aleck loved the private musical world he shared with his mother. The music flowed freely through his fingers when he played beside her. As a boy, Aleck's greatest longing was for a lifelong career in music.

Aleck's father, however, did not share his son's enthusiasm for the piano. He regularly interrupted evening practice sessions to drag Aleck to the living room to participate in scientific talks. "Piano's a fine hobby," Alexander later recalled his father saying, "but never let it get in the way of your serious studies."

Professor Bell hoped the lively scientific living-room discussions would kindle his son's scientific curiosity. Professor Bell made attending seem like a reward. To Aleck it felt a bit more like punishment.

Eliza Bell encouraged her son Aleck's interest in music. She is shown here sitting at the controls of the family velocipede, a type of vehicle that the Bell boys pedaled around town.

Professor Bell had placed himself at the intellectual center of Edinburgh. Colleagues and visiting lecturers gathered at the Bell house for evening talks. Some nights the conversation was held in German. Other nights it was held in Latin. Alexander would helplessly shrug and beg to be excused, saying that he didn't know either German or Latin. His father would growl that Aleck wasted time on dreaming, on wandering, and on music instead of pursuing worthwhile subjects to improve his mind.

WHAT TO DO WITH THE BOY?

Tension gradually mounted in the Bell household over Aleck's development. His mother opened the world of music and art to him. (She was a renowned painter of miniature portraits.) She encouraged his wandering hikes and his

The Rise of Science

An academic and scientific boom swept across Europe in the middle of the 1800s. Edinburgh and its university quickly became an important northern hub of this scientific and engineering revolution—earning Edinburgh the name "Athens of the North." It was a time of stirring leaps forward in discovery and science. While Alexander struggled through his teen years, Louis Pasteur discovered that the growth of yeast is the cause of fermentation and developed his germ theory. Joseph Lister created antiseptic surgery. The rechargeable battery was invented. A transatlantic telegraph line connected London and New York. Four new chemical elements were identified and named. It was a time when new discoveries seemed to leap from behind every corner.

While the other Bell boys liked to joke around, Aleck was considered the biggest clown in the family.

curious musings about the natural world. Alexander's father insisted on disciplined and rigorous study leading to university degrees and a scientific career.

Eleven-year-old Aleck's prime escape was with his older brother, Melly. Aleck was the clown of the family. Any excuse was worth a gag pose in front of their father's new camera. Melly was the only one who appreciated and encouraged Aleck's clownlike nature.

The boys loved to dissect small animals—toads, mice, frogs, birds, cats, and rats. Melly longed to hide dissected organs in little Ted's or in their mother's clothes drawers. Aleck wanted to lay out comparative displays of lungs, skulls, and vocal chords. Their mother encouraged the brothers to sketch the body parts their probing uncovered. Their father countered that their childish play created only dreadful smells and messes and that anything they might learn was already better explained in available textbooks.

Aleck, however, had no enthusiasm for his father's academic world of laboratories, classrooms, and scholarly library research. Textbooks bored him. He believed that a book could teach him nothing that a good hike and some curious probing through nature couldn't teach him better.

"Explore and wonder," urged Aleck's mother.

"Apply yourself with academic and disciplined study," countered his father. And still, Aleck mostly wanted to play with Melly.

Aleck attended the Royal High School in Edinburgh for several years. He is the fourth from the left in the second row from the top.

SEARCHING FOR HIMSELF

Somehow young Alexander had to make sense of the push-pull influences of his mother and his father. He had to find a way to blend them into a single whole that could support his beliefs and his life. But the conflicting forces were difficult for a young dreamer to reconcile. Aleck suffered from sleeplessness and headaches. He wallowed through a long period of fragile health.

Aleck seemed to drift through the closing years of his childhood with no direction, ambition, or purpose. He knew exactly what he liked: music and wandering. But he was also vaguely convinced that he was

Career Choices in the Mid-1800s

Children were not as free to choose their own careers in the mid-1800s as they are today. Then it was common—even expected—that the eldest son would follow in the footsteps of his father and that a father would arrange positions for his other sons. The desires and wishes of the children were not necessarily a significant consideration in making these decisions. What counted were the wishes and mandates of the father.

Professor Bell was unusual in his insistence that all three of his sons follow in his scientific footsteps, not just Melly, the oldest. Most typically, in a family of three sons, the oldest would follow the father, the middle son would enter business or be apprenticed to a trade, and the youngest would enter either the priesthood or the military.

supposed to want something more—something loftier. Young Alexander had no idea of what that might be, though.

Even in those troubled days Alexander never lost his drive for invention or his sense of independence. Alexander was not given a middle name at birth. So he chose one for himself before his eleventh birthday. A friend of Professor Bell's, named Alexander Graham, visited from Canada. Aleck liked the sound of the name and decided he would use a middle name to make himself independent of his father and grandfather. He declared that his middle name was "Graham" and called himself A. Graham Bell, or even just Graham. It made him feel older and more mature. Only when he was romping with Melly did he still feel like an Aleck.

Aleck had to leave his beloved Scotland to move to London to live with grandfather. Aleck's father thought Aleck would have a chance at a better future if he went away.

THREE

Grandfather's Direction

Professor Bell felt determined to see his mischievous son carve out a decent future for himself and believed it would not happen as long as Aleck lingered in Edinburgh. Just before Alexander's fifteenth birthday, in 1862, Professor Bell sent Aleck to live for a year with his grandfather Alexander Bell. Seventy-two-year-old Grandfather Bell lived in London and had recently lost his wife. Grandfather Bell shared the beliefs and attitudes of Professor Bell. He was a strict and demanding man with a stern, scowling face and bushy, snow-white hair. The old man demanded order and discipline and declared of his grandson that "I plan to remedy his defects of education and personal habit."

Grandfather Bell had been a Scottish cobbler who moved to London to be an actor and to teach elocution on the side. Grandfather proudly proclaimed that he had to be an exceptional teacher to get London aristocrats to pay a Scottish cobbler to teach them English elocution.

From the moment Aleck arrived in the teeming metropolis of London, he was forced to dress, speak, behave, think, act, and walk correctly—"with proper decorum." The senior Bell believed that Aleck needed discipline and intensive study and allowed no time for frivolous hobbies, such as playing the piano. Alexander had to take proper afternoon strolls through the twilight haze of London's foul air, looking always like a true gentleman and scholar.

It was a lonely and difficult year for a boy used to romping free and to playing with his brothers. Aleck was separated from Melly, from his mother, from his music, and from his beloved Scottish hills. From sunup until the end of the evening study period, Alexander had to dress in

The Curse of Coal

Steam powered industry, and coal powered steam. Every factory featured tall smokestacks that belched thick, black coal smoke and soot into the air. At that time, factories used no equipment to filter and clean their exhaust. Coal also burned in almost every house to provide heat. England had no pollution-control laws or policies in the 1850s. A thick haze of soot and smoke hung over every industrial city. London's pollution was the worst of all. A layer of grime and black smudge settled daily over everything. Laundry could not be hung for long on outside lines to dry, or it came in grimier than before it was washed. Respiratory illnesses became a common and epidemic danger of urban life.

formal English attire with a high, stiff, starched collar that pushed up hard under both sides of his jaw, rubbing the skin raw. He was forced to wear a waistcoat and either a day coat or evening tails, and he always carried a formal top hat.

Grandfather Bell insisted that Alexander use proper speech, enunciation, and a stately, formal walk rather than the free-swinging strides with which Alexander loped across his Scottish hills. London society was

Aleck missed his home and family terribly. He missed being able to play with his brothers and to spend time with his mother. This photograph shows the Bell boys and their mother in their garden. Edward is the one dressed as a ghost.

a formal and stately affair. The way a young man looked and acted mattered. Grandfather Bell insisted that Alexander look and act the part of a young gentleman.

Six days a week Alexander endured hours of forced study—Shakespeare, Latin, science, speech, and vocalization. Alexander waded through libraries of literature and language and history. Above all, Alexander was made to study the science of sound and speech, that foremost passion of his grandfather and his father. Alexander had to absorb dozens of books on sound.

Alexander had boarded the London-bound train as an eager, curious, undisciplined boy of fourteen. He returned to Edinburgh a year later as a serious, studious, disciplined man of fifteen. He felt "quite grown-up, especially for my age." That one year with his grandfather set Alexander's life direction in cement. Gone were the carefree wandering hikes and musings. Gone was the longing for a career in music. Gone was the drive for play and mischief.

Now Alexander wanted to work, to study, and to achieve noteworthy academic success. His inventive drive and problem-solving skills survived, but they were now focused on the family business of speech. Additionally, his grandfather had sparked a fierce new independence in Alexander, an independence that brought him into frequent clashes with his father.

THE FAMILY BUSINESS

Alexander felt at loose ends after his return to Edinburgh, as if the return were a step backward in his life. He was no longer given the allowance he had come to expect as his rightful due while living in London. He resented being treated like a boy again. He no longer craved quiet hours with his mother. He searched now for meaningful work.

Professor Bell challenged Alexander and Melly to build a talking machine—a working mechanical replica of the human voice apparatus. The boys eagerly dived into the project. With this "talking head," Alexander was determined to prove his worth to his father. After long hours of study, the boys built their mechanical larynx out of tin and rubber. They fashioned jaws, an upper gum, a hard palate, and teeth from hard rubber. They molded a tongue and lips from wood and wire mesh stuffed with cotton and covered with soft rubber. They spent days painstakingly figuring how to make each part move as do the parts of a human vocal apparatus. They used the bellows from a parlor organ for lungs. Wires attached to a keyboard control panel commanded the movement of each part.

Alexander and Melly suffered through more than a hundred design failures before coaxing even the simplest two-letter syllable, "ma," from their machine. Alexander later wrote, "Many times we were discouraged and disheartened over our efforts and ready to give up the whole thing in disgust."

Alexander's determination not to fail in the face of his father drove them on, even after Melly tired of the effort and begged to quit.

Finally it worked. The boys were able to fool neighbors and family into thinking a small child was talking and crying for help. They both delighted in their triumph and in their father's brief nod of recognition.

"The making of this talking machine certainly marked an important point in my career," Bell wrote in 1909. "It made me familiar with the functions of the vocal apparatus, and started me along the path that led to the telephone."

[ENGLISH ALPHABET OF VISIBLE SPEECH,
Expressed in the Names of Numbers and Objects.]

[Pronounce the Nos.] [Names.]	[Name the Objects.]		[Name the Objects.]	
1.				
2.				
3.				
4.				
5.				
6.				
7.				
8.				

[EXERCISE.]

One by one.
Two or three.
Four at once.
Five o'clock.
Half-past six.
Seven-thirty.
Eight to nine.
Ten or twelve.
Twice two, four.
Twice three, six.
Four and four, eight.
Nine and two, eleven.
Twice or thrice.

Two, a couple.
Twelve, a dozen.
Twenty, a score.
A book-case.
A few books.
New book-shelves.
A silver watch.
A gold watch.
The watch-key.
A good saw.
Cap and feather.
Tongs and shovel.
Sugar-tongs.

A hunting whip.
A table lamp.
A bunch of onions.
Corns and bunions.
A ship's boat.
A sailing boat.
Cart and horse.
A round tent.
Rows of houses.
A dog-kennel.
A little monkey.
A pretty cage.
A green canary.

This table shows the names of objects and numbers in Visible Speech, Professor Bell's system for helping deaf and hearing-impaired people to speak.

As a gag, Aleck and Melly decided that it would be great fun to see if they could make the family dog "talk" using their father's concepts for defining and directing speech. Aleck began by teaching it to growl on command. From this basic sound, the boys practiced manipulating the dog's jaw and holding its lips in the correct shape to form various vowel and consonant sounds. They massaged and poked the dog's vocal chords to create resonant tones.

The boys slowly trained the dog to talk. Soon the dog could be made to say a reasonable version of "mama," sounding very much like a young child's cry. Some in the family claimed that the dog sounded better than had their talking machine. They also "taught" the dog to pronounce "ow," "ah," "ga," "gr," and "oo." Their crowning achievement was to get the dog to say "Ow ah oo, gr-ah-ma?" ("How are you, Grandma?")

Friends and neighbors howled with delight and applauded for encores. Professor Bell was not amused. He said that the boys were mocking his work and his theories. The boys were forbidden from

Visible Speech

Professor Bell identified 140 sounds the human vocal apparatus was capable of making and invented symbols to describe the position of each part for each sound. Bell's Visible Speech system used four symbols per sound—one each to describe the position of a speaker's lips, tongue, larynx, and chest, or air flow. Because Visible Speech required so many characters for each sound (even simple three-letter words often used a dozen or more characters), it was a difficult system to learn and master.

continuing their torment of the dog and the neighbors with their mischief.

During the summer of 1864, Professor Bell began to tour extensively, lecturing on his system of Visible Speech. He had cataloged every sound the human vocal system could make and had created symbols to represent the position of the tongue and the lips for each.

Alexander and Melly were taught his system so that, during a lecture, the boys could dramatically be ushered from the room while a guest chose a word or a sound. Professor Bell would write the Visible Speech symbols for the sound on a board. Upon returning, the boys were always able to correctly reproduce the word, though it could have come from any language (even Sanskrit), or even a sound such as a hiss or a yawn—just by reading their father's symbols.

BREAKING AWAY

Alexander, now seventeen, could see the vast potential of Visible Speech to teach the deaf to speak. He had a special interest in the deaf, since his mother was nearly deaf. The thought of dedicating himself to

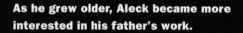
As he grew older, Aleck became more interested in his father's work.

this one project appealed to Alexander. However, he also burned with a growing and powerful craving for independence.

Alexander toyed with the idea of running away to sea, but Melly talked him out of it. Next, Alexander found an ad in a newspaper for two student instructors at Weston House Academy in the far-northern city of Elgin, Scotland—one to teach music and one to teach elocution. Melly agreed to apply too, and the boys secretly submitted their completed applications. Alexander hoped they would be hired and safely away from home before their father learned of the scheme.

The boys, however, made one mistake. They listed their father as a reference on their application forms. The head of Weston House eagerly contacted Professor Bell to discuss the possibility of having his sons teach and study at the school.

While he felt that a teaching post would be a good step for his sons, Professor Bell was angered that his sons had schemed behind his back and embarrassed at being caught unaware. He decided that it was pointless to force Alexander to continue to live at home. Aleck, at least, should go. Melly would stay in Edinburgh as Professor Bell's assistant and would attend classes at the University of Edinburgh as his duties permitted. Alexander would move to Elgin and would have to teach both subjects.

With his own schedule, his own salary, and his first feeling of true independence, Alexander was overjoyed to teach in the Scottish city of Elgin. He taught there for two years, with half a year off in the middle during which he furiously attended advanced classes in Latin, Greek, and physics at the University of Edinburgh—classes he would have refused to touch just two years before. But especially he studied human anatomy of the ear, the mouth, the nose, and the throat.

Alexander wrote a forty-page letter to his father in 1865, during his second year in Elgin. In it he described several experiments he had conducted from which he concluded that faint musical tones could be heard whenever someone uttered any vowel sound. Alexander believed that this was an important link between music and speech.

Impressed by his son's work and thoughts, Professor Bell passed the letter on to linguist Alexander Ellis, considered Europe's leading scientist in the study of language. Ellis sent Alexander a copy of a paper by a German linguist, Hermann von Helmholtz, in which the German concluded the same thing Alexander had noted.

However, Alexander was not proficient in German. From his mistranslation, and from his misinterpretation of the illustrations, Alexander got the impression that von Helmholtz had transmitted vowel sounds electrically over telegraph wires.

Even after Alexander read a proper translation of the paper and learned that von Helmholtz had neither done nor even thought of doing any such thing, the idea of transmitting voice sounds over telegraph wires stuck like a burning ember in Alexander's mind. This "accident" moved Alexander Graham Bell one giant step closer to inventing the telephone.

The
Result of some
Experiments
in connection with
"Visible Speech."
made in
Elgin
in
November 1865

This is the beginning of Aleck's forty-page letter to his father.

Loss Upon Loss

On April 23, 1865, while Alexander lived in Edinburgh, his grandfather died. Melly stayed in Edinburgh, and Professor Bell moved the rest of the family from Edinburgh to London to pick up his father's practice while continuing his own research. That summer, Alexander returned to Elgin to teach.

Alexander expressed little sadness at his grandfather's passing. Perhaps it was because of the distance between them—both physically and emotionally. Perhaps the loss of one family member may have made Alexander feel vulnerable and needing to huddle closer to the others. Whatever his private reasons, when Alexander's teaching contract in Elgin expired, he did not attempt to renew it or to find other work in Scotland.

Alexander searched for a teaching post in England. He found one in Bath, about 100 miles (160 kilometers) west of London. Alexander

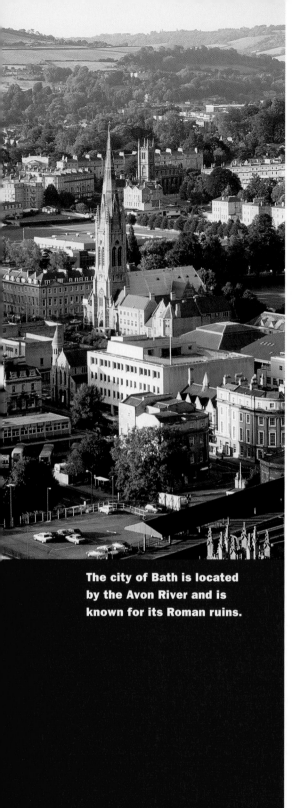

The city of Bath is located by the Avon River and is known for its Roman ruins.

dutifully settled into his new teaching duties and took up long, wandering hikes in his off-hours through the wrinkled Bath hills that led west toward the coastline, the sea, and the fresh salt smell of the ocean. Even from miles away, Alexander said that the faint scent of salt air reminded him of home.

In early 1867, Edward, then eighteen and the tallest of the three boys, fell ill. In May, he died of tuberculosis, prevalent in smoke-choked London. The family trembled at this sudden and cruel loss. A part of the household sparkle disappeared forever with young Ted. Alexander, now twenty, felt more frail and vulnerable than at any other time since he had been a frail boy.

In Bath, Alexander conducted virtually no experiments. He seemed to focus on mere survival and had no energy left for intellectual challenge or investigation.

In 1868 Professor Bell traveled to the United States for an extended lecture tour to promote his Visible Speech.

Alexander had moved to London in the summer of 1867 after he decided not to extend his teaching contract in Bath beyond one year. Rather than seek a third short-term teaching post, he opted to stay in London. He took over his father's practice with private clients while Professor Bell was gone and to "try to fill up the family house," which must have felt quite empty and still with his father away, Melly living in Edinburgh, and Ted gone.

Alexander also worked at the London School for the Deaf two days a week hoping to reenergize his enthusiasm for work. Within a month

Tuberculosis: Death Rattle

Tuberculosis—called consumption in the 1800s—is caused by a bacterium that spread rampantly in industrial urban squalor. Densely packed cities were perfect breeding grounds for infection and disease. London suffered a cholera epidemic in 1855 caused by a lack of sewers. Consumption was also epidemic in London in the 1850s and 1860s. Yet doctors had no cure. Most popular among the many treatments, doctors prescribed sulfur and opium, which did little good, but made patients more comfortable while they slowly withered and died. It would be another fifty years before an effective treatment was discovered. In the mid-1800s, it was not yet understood that germs and bacteria could cause disease, and so consumption was blamed on the damp and coal-choked air of industrial cities. Actually, air pollution did make people more susceptible to consumption and did worsen its effects. The damp air of Edinburgh and London was a perfect medium for transmitting airborne diseases.

of his arrival, Alexander used his father's Visible Speech system to teach a pretty eight-year-old girl who had been born deaf to clearly say, "I love you, Mama."

It was the first sound the girl's mother had ever heard her say. The girl could not hear the sounds she uttered, and still—with Alexander's teaching—she pronounced each word clearly and distinctly. The mother wept with joy and called it "the sweetest sound ever made in the world" and a "miracle beyond all measure." Alexander received much press coverage and fame for this dramatic success.

Parents of deaf children lined up hoping that Alexander could create a similar miracle with their children. Other London educators began to seriously discuss the teaching strategies of this young Bell.

How to Teach the Deaf?

Education for the deaf can be traced to a Spanish Benedictine monk in the 1500s who taught deaf children of nobility to read and speak. This oral education for the deaf spread across Europe and was still common when Professor Bell began his work on Visible Speech. Systematic sign language began with a French monk in the late 1700s and was not well received in Europe, but it spread rapidly throughout the United States once it was introduced by Thomas Hopkins Gallaudet in 1817.

While the world argued about how to teach the deaf to communicate, no one thought it important to also provide a strong, general education for the deaf until Mary Hare started her grammar school for deaf children in England in 1883. Before Hare, the main concerns were to teach the deaf vocational skills and to communicate.

ONE MORE LOSS

Still on his U.S. tour, Professor Bell was amazed to learn that it was Alexander who had become the creator, innovator, and visionary. It was Alexander, whom teachers had scorned—not steady Melly, whom they had praised—who developed ways to apply and extend Visible Speech concepts and theory.

In late 1869, after Professor Bell returned from his triumphant American tour with a satchelful of praise, Melly began to constantly cough in the soot- and smoke-choked damp Edinburgh air. He grew pale, listless, and weak. Unable to work, Melly moved back to London, at the end of April of 1870, to be cared for at home. Alexander watched in horror as his childhood constant companion, his beloved brother, steadily spiraled downhill. Doctors held scant hope for his recovery.

In late May of 1870, Melly died of tuberculosis, just as Ted had three years before. Alexander was overwhelmed by the loss of his coconspirator. He felt that the better part of himself had shriveled and been extinguished. Alexander felt abandoned and frightfully alone. The loss of Ted had been a devastating blow. The loss of Melly struck like a thunderbolt a hundred times harder and deeper.

Work, study, even life itself, held no meaning for the young man who had become a speech and vocal phenomenon. By June, associates noted that Alexander appeared exhausted, weak, and listless. Eliza, deep in her own grief, said that it was due to the loss of Melly. Professor Bell feared that his last son—the one who was becoming the shining academic star he had always hoped for—was succumbing to tuberculosis, as had his brothers.

Professor Bell immediately decided to move the family to a healthier place. He had received many offers for additional lecturing in Canada and the United States. Maybe the air there would be healthier. Maybe in Canada, Alexander could survive.

FLEEING HOME

In July of 1870, Professor Bell placed his family on a ship bound for Canada. It felt like a desperate race to escape the ravages of tuberculosis stalking the London streets and swirling in the foul air.

Friends of Professor Bell arranged for the Bells to rent a house in Brantford, Ontario, a province of Canada. It was a convenient spot while the family searched for a permanent house to buy. They soon purchased a 10-acre (4.05 hectare) farm nearby.

Alexander reluctantly joined his father in this move, feeling that he was abandoning not only Melly but also the countryside he loved and

Professor Bell believed that living in Canada would be healthier for his family.

the students and work that had become his life. To Alexander, the move felt like fleeing, like one more dire loss piled on top of an insurmountable mound of losses. He felt that he was going into hiding, as if he too, were marked for an early death and was now hoping to cheat his doom by cowering behind distant closed shutters.

Invention, electronic development, even new devices and systems to aid the deaf, had been swept from Alexander's mind by his grief. He sank into a lonely, grieving shadow of the carefree boy who had romped across the hills of Scotland. There seemed left in him no energy, no drive.

His mother said that time and the New World would restore Alexander Graham Bell to his happy spirits and onto the path to greatness. Professor Bell's acquaintances in Brantford doubted her optimism. They feared that tuberculosis had sunk its claws into Alexander and that he must surely wither. They feared that the loss of both brothers had stricken him with a terrible grief that would cripple him forever. They feared that his productive life was over.

The idea that Alexander would soon invent the single greatest advance in the history of communications technology—the telephone— seemed no more likely than, say, flying to the moon. The shining promise and potential of Alexander Graham Bell seemed to have flickered, dimmed, and died.

At a school for the deaf in Boston, Alexander employed visible speech to help his deaf students to learn to speak.

FIVE

Boston Beginnings

Alexander languished for four months in Brantford, struggling to regain his strength. He had to find a way to go on with life without Melly and without his homeland. To Alexander, it seemed an impossible task. He could muster neither the will nor the strength to face it.

Professor Bell launched his second U.S. lecture tour. In the fall of 1870, he lectured in Boston. After his rousing talk to an overflow crowd, Professor Bell was approached by Sarah Fuller, who headed the Boston School for Deaf-Mutes. She asked him if he would like to spend several weeks training the teachers of its younger students.

Professor Bell told her that he wasn't interested, but his son, Alexander, would be perfect for the job. Professor Bell signed a contract for Alexander to spend a month teaching the teachers of deaf students in the Boston school.

Alexander returned to teaching lacking the enthusiasm he had felt for his work in London. Still, in April of 1871, at age twenty-four, Alexander moved to Boston to fulfill the contract his father had signed. After his weeks of teaching teachers, Alexander stayed on in Boston, taking a permanent job at the Boston School for the Deaf, teaching his father's Visible Speech system to children who had never heard a sound.

Alexander began his work with each student by sketching a human face, head, neck, and chest on a blackboard. As he touched each drawn part with a pointer, he had students touch the same part of their own bodies. Alexander then erased all parts except those that were essential to speech. Again he had students touch each of these parts while he spoke and demonstrated how he used each part to create speech.

He showed students the position of each body part for each possible sound a human could make. As students began to understand the function of lungs, larynx, throat, tongue, lips, and teeth in the process of speech, Alexander wrote the Visible Speech symbols for each sound on the board. Then he would show students the position of each part of their anatomy for the sound represented by the symbol he had written.

It sounded simple. In practice it was slow, tedious work, leading students to create something they could not hear or even imagine.

Boston educators and parents were astounded by the success Alexander achieved with his father's Visible Speech system. Parents lined up to enroll their children in the school where Alexander taught and to hire him for private lessons for their children. Alexander Graham Bell became a celebrity in Boston society.

Alexander returned to Brantford for the summer of 1871, exhausted but now recharged with a deep fire for work. That summer he translated the Mohawk tribe's language into Visible Speech symbols. In return, they taught him their war dance. At almost every moment of discovery and triumph through the rest of his life, Alexander Graham Bell spontaneously broke into that dance—not a war dance for Alexander but one of joy, renewed life, and creation.

Still, Alexander struggled to make ends meet. Teachers were poorly paid in the late 1800s, and teachers of disabled students received the lowest pay of all. Moreover, most parents were unwilling to offer more than a pittance for private lessons.

School Time in Boston

Massachusetts, in general, and Boston, in particular, had strong programs for public education. In 1852, Massachusetts passed a law that required children between the ages of eight and fourteen to attend school for at least twelve weeks each year. The law, however, was not strictly enforced.

In the decade following the Civil War, the great educational concern was how best to integrate the flood of southern blacks into the educational system. In many areas blacks were given separate schools. "Separate" usually meant inferior teachers and inferior facilities.

With the repercussions of the Civil War and slavery still rolling through every aspect of life in the United States, education for disabled students was pushed to a very low priority. Teachers of the deaf were given bottom-rung pay. It was expected that deaf students would be taught only to communicate, and they were often completely ungraded in any school subject.

HIS OWN SCHOOL

Back in Boston, Alexander continued his teaching and attended lectures at the Massachusetts Institute of Technology (MIT), then only a few years old. Professor Lewis Monroe, a noted linguist, allowed Alexander to use MIT lab equipment for his experiments. The fancy equipment at the university was a godsend for the young experimenter barely able to afford rent and food.

Alexander decided that private clients would pay better if he were not associated with an established school. Besides, private clients could serve as subjects for his speech experiments. He quit his teaching job, rented rooms in Boston, and opened the School of Vocal Physiology. His advertisements promised that he could correct "stammering, stuttering, and other defects of utterance." The sign he hung next to the door bragged PRACTICAL, PROVEN INSTRUCTION IN VISIBLE SPEECH.

One of his first clients was five-year-old George Sanders, son of wealthy leather merchant Thomas Sanders. George had been

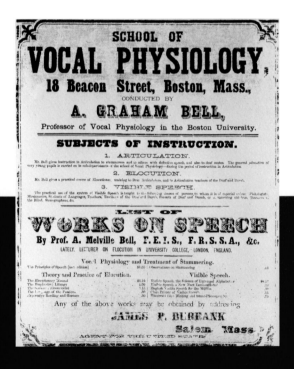

After returning to Boston, Alexander decided to start his own business. This is an advertisement for Alexander's new venture, the School of Vocal Physiology.

born deaf. Being only five, George could not yet read—an essential step in learning the Visible Speech system. Alexander couldn't afford to lose a lucrative client, so he invented a "magic glove" for George to wear. Alexander printed the twenty-six letters in easy-to-touch spots on the glove. Both George and Alexander could point to the appropriate letters to form words and communicate as an alternative to writing and reading while George learned to speak.

Thomas Sanders was thrilled with the progress George made under his new teacher. He became a fan of Alexander's and would, in a few years, be one of Alexander's prime financial backers in the development of the telephone.

THE RETURN TO INVENTION

In late 1872, the Western Union Telegraph Company announced that it had purchased an invention that would allow telegraph operators to send two messages simultaneously over the same wire. It was a major advance since before, each telegram tied up the telegraph lines for many minutes and made telegrams costlier than ordinary citizens could afford.

The announcement rekindled Alexander's passion for invention. He dreamed of inventing a system to allow many messages to be sent simultaneously over a single telegraph wire.

Before the telegraph, news had to be literally carried by horse, carriage, train, or ship, or on foot. It could take a week or more for important news to reach New York from New Orleans, for example. With the telegraph, suddenly the news could be delivered in seconds. To the public it was astounding, almost unimaginable.

The problem with telegraphs was that Morse code, the language of dots and dashes transmitted over telegraph lines, was too slow. A long word could take twenty seconds to send and receive. A single sentence could take a minute. A long news article sent to a newspaper by a field

Morse's Magic

Early telegraphs were simple, battery-powered electrical circuits very similar to the circuit that makes a flashlight work. Until a switch is pushed to "on," no electricity flows from the flashlight battery, and the light doesn't light. When the switch is turned on, the electrical current flows, and the flashlight lights. If the switch were rapidly clicked on-off-on-off, the flashlight's light would pulse so that someone far away could see and count the pulses of light.

The circuit between two telegraph stations worked the same way. It was normally open, which meant that no electrical current flowed down the line. When an operator at one end tapped on a round disk called a key, he pushed two strips of metal together that completed the circuit—similar to turning the flashlight on—allowing electricity to flow down the telegraph wire to the distant station. An operator at the distant end could hear the telegraph circuit click on, just as someone could see a flashlight turn on. If one operator tapped on his key in a rhythmic pattern, the distant operator would hear that pattern at his station as a series of clicks. Samuel Morse developed a telegraph machine, and he used a code of short taps called dots and long taps called dashes to represent every letter and number. A sending operator would tap out the one to four dots and dashes for every letter or symbol in a message. The receiving operator would hear those dots and dashes as clicks and write down the message letter by letter.

correspondent could tie up the system for hours. Important telegraphs would often have to wait a day or more to be able to get onto the line since only one message at a time could be transmitted.

For a system of instant communications, telegraphs were slow and expensive. A one-page telegram often cost hundreds of dollars to send. Newspapers and the government were the only users who could regularly afford the telegraph. However, if Western Union Telegraph Company and the other telegraph companies could find a way to send multiple messages over a line, prices would drop dramatically, and businesses and private citizens could afford telegraphs.

From his study of sound, Alexander knew that, when he hit a tuning fork, the sound vibration it produced would make a piano wire or a second tuning fork also vibrate if it was tuned to the same note or frequency as the first tuning fork. However, it would not make any other piano wire or tuning fork vibrate.

Alexander began to wonder if tuning forks and telegraphs could be combined. If he could find a way to transmit the tone, or note, of a tuning fork down a telegraph line, then that tone should make a tuning fork on the other end also vibrate. If he interrupted the vibrations of his tuning fork with a Morse code pattern of dashes and dots, then the distant tuning fork should click on and off, its vibrations reproducing the same Morse code message on the other end.

If Alexander could send one message down a telegraph line from one tuning fork to another, then he should be able to send a second message down the same wire if he sent it between two separate tuning forks tuned to a different frequency. The tuning forks would not affect each other since they weren't tuned to the same frequency. If he could send two messages down the same line, then he should be able to send hundreds of signals down a single wire, each carried on its own, unique pitch or frequency between its own pair of tuning forks. At the far end of the wire, tuning forks that matched the vibrational tone of each signal would begin to vibrate and recreate the dots and dashes sent along each individual tone.

Bell called his idea a harmonic telegraph. He added "harmonic" because he would use the harmonic tones of his tuning forks to create the tones to carry each of his telegraph signals down the same wire. The idea was very similar to the many television channels that are transmitted down a single cable today, each carried on its own separate frequency called a carrier frequency. Because carrier frequencies are different, television channels don't interfere with each other. Similarly, Bell reasoned that the harmonic tones he would use as his carriers would not interfere with each other.

It felt wonderful to be consumed by the drive to invent. Alexander, however, didn't understand electrical engineering—modern science calls it electronics—well enough to know if it was possible to make his idea work. Neither did he know engineering well enough to see that his harmonic telegraph would be only one small step away from a telephone.

Alexander's life flowed into a steady whirlwind rhythm: teach during the day, give private lessons in the afternoon and evening, conduct experiments late at night, and attend lectures on the weekends. Like a hound on the hunt, Alexander sniffed steadily along the trail chasing the elusive harmonic telegraph without guessing that this same trail would lead instead to the telephone.

Many inventors were scrambling to create multiple telegraphs. Alexander knew that his progress was too slow to win the race for discovery and invention. To be the first with a working harmonic telegraph, he needed abundant time and money—neither of which he had.

SIX

The Move to Invention

If Alexander Graham Bell could make his harmonic telegraph work, every telegraph company would want to install his system on every telegraph line in the country—in the world. He'd sell thousands. He'd make a fortune if he could make it work.

The harmonic telegraph, of course, had no direct connection with his work of teaching the deaf to speak. Still, Bell justified turning much of his time and attention toward the telegraph by telling himself that the original idea for it arose from his long-term study of sound and human hearing and speech.

Even with the excitement of discovery roaring in his ears, Bell's work became increasingly scattered. In 1873 he started a magazine, *The Visible Speech Pioneer*, which found only limited success. His teenage idea of transmitting voice over telegraph lines popped back into his head, demanding its share of attention. He began his first small experiments with voice transmission as well as simple tone transmission for his telegraph.

Bell's teaching also continued. In 1873, he was offered a teaching post at the University of Boston, which he eagerly accepted, thrilled that he, a Scot without a college degree, would be lecturing at an American university.

In the constant rush of activity, it was difficult for Bell to find a common, unifying thread in all his projects or to remember his general purpose and goals. Bell toiled frantically through 1873 and 1874—working long into every night—just to keep each of his efforts afloat. It seemed that he was desperately trying to erase the memory of his grandfather's scoldings and to prove himself worthy to his father and to the memory of Melly—or maybe just to prove his worth to himself.

During this frenzied period, Bell met Mabel Hubbard, the daughter of Gardiner Hubbard, a lawyer and president of the Clark School for the Deaf. He wanted Alexander to make his daughter speak clearly. She could lip-read, but her speech was slurred and indistinct. A bout of scarlet fever when she was five had left Mabel totally deaf. She came to Alexander as a student when he was twenty-six and she was nearly sixteen.

Mabel described her new teacher as "quick, enthusiastic, and interesting, but careless in his dress with his horribly shiny broadcloth, very conceited and altogether, I did not think him exactly a gentleman."

By early 1874, however, she wrote to her mother, "Mr. Bell said today my voice was naturally sweet. . . I am sure he continues pleased with me." She decided that she "did not dislike him."

For his part, Alexander thought of Mabel only as a student, as a voice to be taught and tested, until their lives slowly intertwined during the next year. Rather than describing Mabel when he wrote to his parents in early 1874, Bell reported only how pleased he was to be a professor at a university and to be a guest lecturer at MIT: "[It] has placed me in a new position in Boston. It has brought me in close contact with the scientific minds of the city."

Bell had become his father and grandfather, swirling in the center of an important city's academic circle—Boston. This was not a bad thing. Both earlier Bells were successful and did important work. But something was missing for Alexander. He had pleased his father, but not yet himself. He had not honored his call to invent.

INCHING TOWARD INVENTION

Through early 1874, Bell's experiments and thoughts were scattered across a wide range of inventive ideas—the musical quality of vowels, the harmonic telegraph, the nature of sounds and speech, and some initial stages of his work on voice transmission. Rather than concentrate on one of these, he soon added yet another device he wanted to explore. Bell believed that the phonautograph—a machine

Mabel Hubbard lost her hearing at a young age. At first, Bell considered her only as one of his students, but later she would win his heart. She is shown here around the time of her marriage to Bell.

that drew the shapes of sounds by tracing their vibrations with pens—could help the deaf see what sounds looked like and could show when they correctly created the sounds of proper speech. He hoped to make the device easier to use and clearer in the feedback it provided to a deaf speaker.

Each evening Bell rushed to a bevy of experiments on his various ideas, never sure of exactly what he hoped to accomplish or of whether he was even making any real headway. He jumped from one project to another as a new thought sprang into his mind, not bothering to finish the experiment he had just started. Like a juggler spinning more and more plates—each balanced on a wobbly pole—Bell frantically bounced from project to project, spinning each just enough to keep it from crashing.

In the last half of 1874, several of his separate ideas began to fit together. His work to assemble an improved phonautograph showed Alexander that sound was made up of a complex series of simple pressure waves in the air. It gave him the idea that

This is Bell's phonautograph. This device was supposed to help deaf people better understand speech by creating visual images of sounds.

he might be able to make an electric current vary—not just from on to off as in a telegraph but also from tiny to large, and through all levels in between. If so, he should be able to vary the size of an electric current to exactly match the size of a sound vibration in the air.

If he could do that, this continuously rising and falling electric current would exactly match the way sound waves of human speech rise and fall in the air. If he could send that varying electrical signal to the far end of a telegraph line, there it could—somehow—be turned back into sound waves in the air. Inventors Elisha Gray and Thomas Edison called such a projected device a talking telegraph. Alexander Graham Bell, following the terminology created by German inventor Philip Reis, called it a telephone.

But how to do it? That he still didn't know. There were too many ifs and too few answers to give Alexander much hope of success.

That same winter Bell decided that a telephone would need two separate electrical devices. One, the transmitter, would change physical sound waves into electrical current and transmit the current down a wire. The other, the receiver, would receive the electrical signal and change it back into physical sound waves.

Bell realized that his transmitter would have to mimic a human ear. An ear converts acoustic sound waves into electrical pulses. His transmitter would have to do the same—except that it would send the signal not to a brain but down an electrical telegraph wire to a distant receiver. That gave Bell the idea to use a soft rubber membrane (like an eardrum) that could make some fluid behind it vibrate (as does the fluid of the human inner ear). Then he would have to find a way to convert liquid vibrations into an electrical signal, just as the tiny hairs of the inner ear do.

Bell felt that he was finally making progress. These advances led his dreams away from a harmonic telegraph—where he felt blocked and frustrated trying to send a tone of any kind down an electrical wire—and toward a telephone. But that shift only created a whole new set of puzzling questions. What equipment would convert sound waves to electrical current? How should he connect and power his transmitter? What should the receiver be made of? If his transmitter was going to mimic a human ear, should his receiver mimic human vocal chords? How would it convert electrical vibrations back into audible sound?

The concept of a telephone was exciting. But it created nothing but questions and problems for Alexander that seemed even more insurmountable than those that plagued his harmonic telegraph.

BELL AND WATSON

Bell was beginning to form a general design of a working telephone. But he needed dedicated time to develop the concept—full days of time, weeks and months of time. If Alexander were to become a true inventor, he needed to stop doing his father's work—using Visible Speech to teach the deaf to talk—and invent! He also needed engineering expertise. Both needs could be met only with money.

Gardiner Hubbard and Thomas Sanders provided the answer. Both were wealthy and well connected in Boston and New York financial circles. Both had deaf children with whom Alexander had done wondrously well. The two men pledged to back Bell's inventive work. In February 1875, they formed the Bell Patent Association. However, Hubbard and Sanders specifically told Bell that their interest lay with the harmonic telegraph and that that was the only work they wanted to support. Bell agreed to this to secure their funding—even though he had no intention of dropping his work on the telephone.

Bell moved his equipment and experiments to new rented quarters in Boston. He stopped his teaching and most of his lecturing, and he let go of many of his private clients. Of course, George Sanders, now eight, and Mabel Hubbard, now almost eighteen, were two students Alexander continued to work with on a regular basis.

Bell understood sound. He understood human speech and hearing anatomy and function. But he still did not know mechanical and electrical engineering well enough to make the kind of progress his investors demanded. He was admittedly clumsy and lacked manual dexterity. He complained that he had difficulty working with small tools, wires, and pieces of machinery. Everything mechanical took Bell far longer than it was expected to.

Thomas Watson was an invaluable help to Bell. Watson poses with the invention that resulted from his work with Bell— the telephone.

Hubbard discovered that Elisha Gray, an engineer and inventor working in Chicago with Western Union Telegraph Company backing, hotly pursuing the invention of both a harmonic telegraph and a voice telegraph. There could be only one winner in this race to fame, fortune, and glory. He who hesitated or stalled in his research would surely lose.

It was time for outside help. One day in 1874, Bell met engineer Thomas Watson—then just twenty and working for the Charles Williams

Elisha Gray: Inventor

Born in Ohio in 1835, Elisha Gray became fascinated with electricity while studying engineering at Oberlin College. In 1867 he invented an improved telegraph relay, an invention that began his long association with the Western Union Telegraph Company.

Gray worked simultaneously on a harmonic telegraph and a voice telegraph (telephone) for Western Union in 1875 and early 1876. Even though Gray entered the spring of 1876 with a telephone design that seemed to be ahead of Bell's design, it was Alexander Bell who transmitted the first human speech over a telephone. It was Bell who rocked the world with his telephone demonstration at the Centennial Exposition that June, while Gray had not yet been able to make his telephone work.

Though he received more than seventy patents for electrical devices (including the harmonic telegraph) and founded the successful Western Electric Manufacturing Company, Gray remained bitter and resentful of Bell's telephone coup.

Electrical Supply Company—when Bell stormed into Williams's shop to complain about the design of a mechanical part he had ordered.

The two men talked about Bell's work and his plans. Watson was impressed with Bell's knowledge of sound and with his infectious and intense enthusiasm. Bell was impressed with Watson's calm and deliberate mechanical mind and with his solid understanding of electricity. The two connected immediately.

Watson became a part-time assistant of Bell's, retaining his position at the Williams company with the rest of his time. The pair agreed to concentrate on creating a harmonic telegraph and on sending tones down a telegraph wire that would cause a tuning fork at the receiving station to vibrate. Watson felt that tones would be easier than an actual voice to transmit. Besides, the harmonic telegraph was the invention Hubbard and Sanders thought had a good chance to make a profit for their partnership. Still, Bell was daily drawn to gaze at his notes and ideas for a telephone. He just couldn't make himself set it aside.

The weeks raced toward the hot, muggy summer of 1875, a summer when it was time to either succeed or fade away in the failed dreams of science could-have-beens. If Bell didn't succeed soon, surely Elisha Gray would. And still, nothing Bell and Watson tried had worked.

Bell and Watson worked on their experiments on the top floor of this building in Boston.

SEVEN

The Watson Connection

The stifling mugginess of June 2, 1875, in Boston made even breathing seem an unbearable effort in the cramped attic of Charles Williams's shop, which Bell had rented as a laboratory and where he and Watson had struggled all morning. But now Watson wanted to stop. Heat made Bell grumpy, irritable, and even more impatient than usual. Watson suggested that they take the afternoon off.

Bell glared, raised a heavy eyebrow, and solemnly shook his head. During his later lecture tours, Watson claimed that Bell responded that June day by saying, "A day off is a luxury we can't afford."

Someone was going to make a harmonic telegraph work. He who won the race would be famous and rich. He who came in second would be forgotten. That was the way of science. Besides, what would Hubbard and Sanders say if they lost the race?

After two months in the ovenlike attic, the two men still couldn't send anything but "clicks" down an electrical line, and Morse had done that forty years ago. By now even Thomas Watson was tired of the seemingly endless hunt for solutions—hunts that always ended in new problems.

Yes, Bell and Watson had managed to send two signals down a single telegraph line at the same time using separate transmitters and receivers for each circuit. Yes, it was a big step forward. But Bell was committed to creating a harmonic telegraph capable of carrying hundreds of signals at one time.

Bell had even demonstrated his two-channel telegraph for the Western Union Telegraph Company in May, hoping they would want to purchase the design from him and ease his money pressures. It turned out Western Union wasn't serious about considering Bell's design. Rather, it wanted to steal his ideas and give them to Elisha Gray, already working on both a harmonic telegraph and a talking telegraph for the company.

So now Bell pressed hard to show that he could send three independent simultaneous signals through the same wire in order to prove that he had a workable idea for a harmonic telegraph. Bell was impatient to make this design work and to get on to something grand.

After a brief noontime pause, Bell returned to finish connecting their latest design for sending three simultaneous circuits over the wire to the three tuned receivers in the other room, one for each of the three transmitters.

In the transmitting, or sending, room Bell and Watson had stacked large batteries, spools of wire, and the equipment they hoped would change speech into electrical currents. From the transmitting room, a wire ran to the hearing, or receiving, room. Here sat more bulky rectangular batteries, magnets, boxes of fabric, felt diaphragms stretched over metal canisters that Bell had hoped to make vibrate with an electric current, and scattered tools and other devices that he had tried at one time or another in his efforts to change electrical currents back into air-pressure waves.

In the room with his three circuits to connect, Watson felt the pressing heat and frustration that had been building for days. What was there for him to do that they hadn't already tried? That hadn't already failed?

He toyed with magnetic metal reeds (one possible option for use as circuit tuning forks) and with a canister filled with charcoal granules that had long wires trailing out of two sides. They had thought to use this fist-sized device as part of the circuit that changed sound waves into electrical current but had never tested it.

Watson later wrote, "It was a day . . . of vivid contrasts—a black and white, gloom and sunshine, lean and fat, poverty and riches sort of a day."

The two men had endured the black, lean, gloomy poverty of the morning—actually, an apt characterization for most of the past week. Now it was time for the sun to shine for them, starting that afternoon.

PLUCKING ON REEDS

To transmit three telegraph messages over the same wire, each circuit, or channel, had to be driven by its own tuning fork vibrating at its own frequency. But if Bell chose the wrong frequencies for each of these three circuits, the combined vibrations of the forks—like the combined notes of a musical chord—could create harmonic vibrations that would inadvertently vibrate the tuning forks when they weren't supposed to be vibrating.

Bell needed to find frequencies to use for each circuit that would not interfere with the others. Musically, he needed to find dissonant notes that would not form any combined harmonics that might cause one fork to affect another. Bell was forced to endure a cacophony of caterwauling noise as he experimented with different note combinations searching for perfect dissonance. To the sensitive ear of a trained musician this noise grated like fingernails down a blackboard. The heat and delays had given Bell a headache. The dissonant twanging turned it into a pounding monster.

Frustrated and irritated, Bell strode down the hall to see if Watson was ready in the receiving room. Yes, the receivers would be ready as soon as Bell adjusted each metal reed of the receiving tuning forks to match the frequencies he had picked in the transmitting room.

Adjustments complete, Bell marched back to the bedroom. There he connected batteries to power the transmitter and struck the metal-reed tuning fork of the first circuit. Watson stepped into the hall and called that he had received vibrational clicks on circuit number one. Bell repeated the test with circuit number two and got the same satisfying result. He sent the third circuit's frequency through the wire. But in Watson's room nothing happened. The failure of something simple that should not have failed had become a gallingly familiar occurrence. Bell slammed down a pair of pliers, rubbed his weary face, and stomped down the hall.

Did the receiving reed touch its electromagnet? Was the reed not gapped correctly? Had Watson checked the pitch of the balky receiver? Was there a wire not tightened?

After a cursory check, Bell returned to the transmitting room, ordering Watson to work on that faulty receiver. Watson disconnected the circuit's power source and adjusted the screw on its contact point. Looking for something else to do, he wired the compressed carbon canister into the circuit and changed from the regular metal reed to the magnetic metal reed they had never tested.

Watson plucked the new reed as he adjusted its tension and gap. Sweat dripped off his face. Idly he plucked and adjusted.

EUREKA!

Alexander burst back into the hot room, his face flushed. "Watson, what did you do?" he demanded.

Embarrassed at being caught idling, Watson confessed that he had been fanning himself and plucking the reed instead of working.

Bell commanded Watson to do it again.

At first Watson was confused, not sure of what he was to repeat. Then Bell exclaimed that he had heard notes—musical notes—that Watson had played instead of mere clicks. He had heard notes through the reeds of his transmitter! The reed in Bell's transmitter for that third circuit had vibrated all by itself. Somehow, by twanging his metal reed over the electromagnet for that circuit, Watson sent a weak electrical current down the line to make Bell's reed vibrate with the same musical note—even though there was no power source connected to it!

The heat was instantly forgotten. Both men eagerly poured over the circuit Watson had absent-mindedly wired together while searching for the one magic change that they had never made before.

Bell recognized the magnetic reed. He had had the idea to try one more than a year earlier but had never tested it, afraid the current it produced would be too weak to travel to a receiver. The canister was one they had filled with activated charcoal. Charcoal was carbon, and compressed carbon could easily carry a weak electrical signal.

The magnetic reed created a magnetic field. When the reed vibrated, its magnetic field also vibrated. That vibrating—or changing—magnetic field induced a matching electrical current to flow through the electromagnetic coil of wire next to it. That current was carried and amplified by the compressed charcoal granules and then transmitted to Bell's bedroom receiver.

Making a Phone Talk

There are four parts to a telephone: the receiver (earpiece), the transmitter (mouthpiece), a ringer system, and the line. Electrical impulses reaching the receiver create a magnetic field that pulls on (vibrates) a thin metal diaphragm. These vibrations create physical sound waves that are transmitted to the ear. In a transmitter, sound waves compress carbon granules to increase or decrease the flow of electricity. In older, rotary-dial phones, you can unscrew the plastic cover over the mouthpiece to remove and examine this canister of carbon granules.

One pair of wires connects your phone to a local switchboard. Both your voice and that of the person you are talking to are carried over this one pair of wires. The two voices are kept separate because each is carried on a different carrier frequency (just as in Bell's harmonic telegraph).

This circuit did not transmit just on-and-off clicks. It transmitted notes, sounds. Bell and Watson had just taken the first huge step toward making a telephone work!

In Bell's mind the harmonic telegraph was instantly set aside, replaced by the splendid prospect of inventing a working telephone. He felt confident that they had finally found the missing piece to convert mechanical energy (sound waves) into electrical energy in his telephone transmitter. It was so simple, so obvious in hindsight. Why had it taken them long months and hundreds of trials to finally reach the answer?

Bell believed that he could finally make electrical signals mirror the vibrational patterns of simple sounds. Now he had to improve his sending (or talking) unit enough to be able to reproduce the complex patterns of speech and then refine the corresponding receiver unit.

On the afternoon of June 2, it all seemed quite simple and doable. Bell thought that he was only days away from ultimate success, from creating a working telephone. In reality, nine months later he still would not be able to transmit a single word.

All of Bell and Watson's hard work on the telephone was beginning to pay off in the summer of 1875. This portrait of Bell was taken the year before the birth of the telephone.

EIGHT

The Pressure Is On

The door to the telephone had cracked open. Bell and Watson had transmitted not just a click but a tone—a musical note—through an electric wire. That very afternoon of June 2, 1875, Bell and Watson drew up a design for their telephone transmitter.

Bell glowed with self-satisfied elation. But he also felt immensely guilty. His investors were paying him to create a harmonic telegraph. He kept reporting to them that he was working on a harmonic telegraph—but making little progress.

He wondered how he would announce this glorious development on the telephone without giving away the lie he had been living. He carefully worded a letter to Gardiner Hubbard: "Dear Mr. Hubbard, I have accidentally made a discovery of the very greatest importance."

Hubbard ignored the letter and dismissed the progress on a telephone as meaningless. He saw an immediate and desperate need for the harmonic telegraph and knew that it would create profit. Like many at the time, Hubbard considered the telephone as an unnecessary, frivolous toy. He felt that the telephone was a risky whim while the harmonic telegraph was a sure winner. Bell, who so clearly saw the potential of the telephone, felt that he was being squeezed in a vise.

That summer and fall was the most stressful period of Bell's life. He felt intense pressure from his investors. Elisha Gray was making steady progress on his harmonic telegraph and also on his talking telegraph. Watson fell ill and was confined to bed for three months. Bell also suffered illness, but he kept to his usual schedule. Working alone, Bell made no significant progress on either his telephone or telegraph.

Bell also suffered a severe financial pinch. He had spent the money provided by his backers and was earning virtually nothing since he had closed his school and stopped most private clients. He felt that he couldn't go begging to Hubbard because he realized (with a sizable shock) that he was deeply in love with Mabel. He didn't dare appear financially irresponsible to the man he hoped would be his future father-in-law.

In July, Bell wrote to his parents, "I am eleven years her senior and look much older than I am. In her youth I fear she will not reciprocate my feelings." His parents agreed that she wouldn't and added sternly that he couldn't possibly consider marriage, since he lacked the means to support a wife. Actually, they opposed the marriage because they feared having deaf children in the family.

In October, Bell felt encouraged when he shifted from steel springs to a thin rubber membrane as the vibrating element in his telephone receiver and noted a marked improvement in the quality of received tones.

Hubbard was not impressed. He ordered Bell to give up on the telephone and finish the harmonic telegraph. It was both a command and a threat.

Bell didn't dare to argue because he was almost ready to ask for Mabel's hand. Still he secretly continued to work on the telephone at least as much as on the telegraph. Bell's guilt and dread increased as he envisioned some future explosive confrontation with Hubbard and Sanders when the truth finally came out. But his fevered excitement also steadily increased. He knew he was close to making a telephone work and could almost taste sweet success.

This is a prototype of the telephone that Bell made in 1875.

In early November, Alexander summoned all his courage and asked for Mabel's hand. They were formally engaged on Thanksgiving Day, 1875—Mabel's birthday. Mabel asked Alexander to drop the *k* from *Aleck* as an engagement present. She thought *Alec* looked more "American." He agreed.

FROM PATENT TO TELEPHONE

By January of 1876, Hubbard wanted to patent Bell's telegraph and telephone designs to protect the devices. Bell replied that he couldn't apply for a patent for a machine until he could make it work. Hubbard countered, "If you don't secure a patent soon, someone else will and your work will be worthless."

On the morning of February 14, and without Bell's knowledge, Hubbard filed the patent application in Bell's name for "unique improvements in the area of voice transmission on a telegraph," which described Bell's telephone design. Hubbard had heard that Thomas Edison—as well as Elisha Gray and another group in Denmark—were close to filing their own applications. Hubbard did not intend to be the second to file. The patent would go to the first legitimate applicant, and only the patent holder would amass the vast economic rewards it would bring.

As fate would have it, two hours later on that exact same day of February 14, Elisha Gray filed a patent caveat for his talking telegraph in Washington, D.C. A caveat is a notice of intent to file soon for a patent for an invention. It's a claim that the inventor has had a specific idea and is close to making it work. It's a warning to others not to horn in on this invention.

If Hubbard hadn't filed that very morning, Elisah Gray would have stood first in line to receive the telephone patent. Any chance Bell would have had when he later filed his own patent applications would have depended in part on showing that Gray's system, as filed in the caveat, wouldn't work. If he failed to show that, Bell could have patented only those parts of his system that were substantially different from Gray's. If Hubbard hadn't filed the patent application that morning, it might well be the Gray Telephone Company, not the Bell system, that we now use.

Gray had developed a complete theory and mechanical design for a telephone but hadn't been able to transmit a voice signal. He believed it unethical to file an actual patent application until he had demonstrated

U.S. Patents

A patent grants exclusive rights to an inventor to produce, use, and sell his or her invention. To handle the rush of claims for patent rights, the U.S. government set up a patent office in 1836 to examine applications and grant patents. During the nineteenth century, more than ten thousand applications were received each year. Each applicant had to either demonstrate his or her invention for the patent office officials or describe on paper what he or she had invented, show how it was significantly new and different from what was already available, and declare that his or her invention infringed on no existing patent. Most applicants failed the test and were rejected. Still, more than three thousand patents a year were issued.

his design. In fact, as of mid-February, he was ahead of Bell in the telephone's development.

On March 7, patent number 174,465 for "Improvement in Telegraphy" was granted to Alexander Graham Bell—and he still hadn't been able to transmit a single word of speech. If Bell couldn't produce a working telephone soon, it would be not only a disaster but also a fraud. Certainly Bell did not intend to defraud anyone. But his filed and sworn patent application claimed that he had a working instrument.

To Bell, March 10, 1876, dawned just like any other in the long line of stressful days spent beating his head against a stone wall, hoping for a miraculous breakthrough. He was testing a new acid-based, variable-resistance liquid transmitter unit. Watson was down the hall in their new quarters at 5 Exeter Place, which Bell had rented in January. As Bell tightened the electrical connections to this unit, he spilled acid across his sleeve and arm. Smoke swirled as fabric and skin burned.

This is a page from Bell's notebook on the work he and Watson did on the telephone on March 10, 1876.

Without thinking, Bell pushed the transmit button and called, "Mr. Watson, come here. I want to see you."

Watson raced down the hall shouting, "I heard you! I heard you!"

The mild acid burn was forgotten. The men spent the rest of the evening giddily talking from room to room using the new transmitter unit. For the night of March 10, laughter, self-congratulations, and the joy of sweet success were enough. Tomorrow was soon enough to analyze just what made this transmitter work.

Bell was flooded with an overwhelming sense of relief. The stress melted away. The impossible hurdle had been overcome. Bell could at last transmit voices down a telegraph wire. The patent and patent application were no longer a lie. Bell's telephone worked!

SHOWING IT TO THE WORLD

By mid-March, Bell wrote to his father, "The day is coming when [telephone] wires will be laid onto houses just like water or gas [lines]—and friends will converse with each other without leaving home." But Bell still had not publicly demonstrated his telephone, and he was terrified of the thought of facing scientific and press criticism. Bell was especially terrified of facing the scientific competition at the Centennial Exposition in Philadelphia, the grand national exposition of American technology as the country turned one hundred years old. Bell's fiancée and father-in-law-to-be pushed him the hardest into showing the world his new invention at the Philadelphia exposition.

June 23 through June 26 was designated as the time for judging all electric exhibits at the fair. Hubbard demanded that Bell set up a booth

The Centennial Exposition

The first one hundred years had been turbulent and shaky for the fledgling United States. American soil had been stained red with the blood of the Revolutionary War, the War of 1812, and the Civil War, each of which had threatened to tear the nation apart. The Centennial Exposition was also called the International Exhibition of Arts, Manufactures and Products of the Soil and Mine, held in Philadelphia, and it was designed to celebrate the nation's survival and to showcase America's best and brightest scientific achievements. The Centennial Exposition was an important chance for the United States to boast about its technological and inventive prowess, to show the world how great a nation it was.

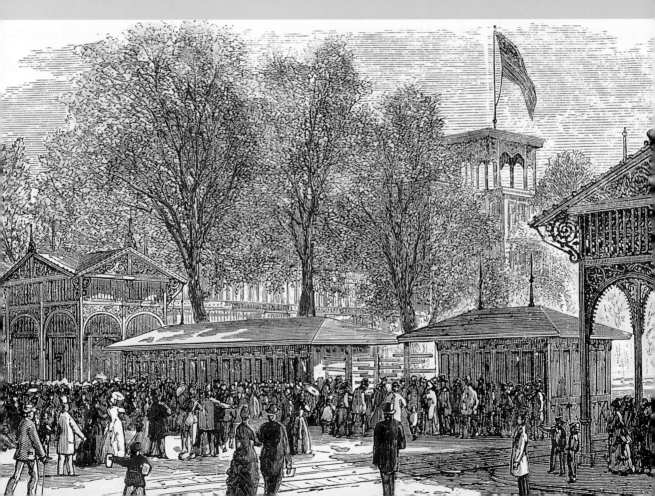

and enter the fray with his completed telephone and nearly completed harmonic telegraph.

Elisha Gray was there with his working harmonic telegraph. Edison was there with several of his recent wonders. More than 130 booths of electric exhibits lined the Main Exhibition Building that stretched over 1,880 feet (573 meters) and was decked with red, white, and blue streamers from end to end.

Elisha Gray, with Western Union funding, held center court on the main floor near the great double doors in an elaborate triple booth. Bell was stuck in a corner of the second floor and set up on one bare folding table. He feared (and secretly hoped) that no one—including the judges—would find or notice his display. Some of his equipment had been damaged in transit. Even after frenzied repairs, Bell feared it wouldn't work as it had in his Boston lab.

The day wore on, hot and muggy, as the judges and a crowd of followers ambled down the main aisle, examining each invention, questioning the inventors, scribbling hurried notes on their clipboard pads. With only forty minutes left before the judges were scheduled to leave, they had covered the first floor and less than half of the second. Most of the judges had already wandered back downstairs to escape the stuffiness of the second floor.

Several honored dignitaries who were familiar with Visible Speech noticed Bell hiding in the crowd during one of Elisha Gray's final demonstrations. With loud greetings, two of them—and especially Dom Pedro, the emperor of Brazil—herded Bell back to his booth to show off his devices, gathering scattered judges as they went, demanding that they all review Bell's display.

Thus, in the very final moments of the competition, with his chance for recognition and fame almost gone, it was a Brazilian monarch who snatched triumph from defeat for Bell. Bell had given up and was ready to pack up his equipment and slink back to Boston without being judged. Dom Pedro made sure he did not.

Bell thoroughly described both the theory and the function of his telephone and demonstrated it for the judges. Dom Pedro demanded to try the device. With a look of reverent awe he declared Bell's telephone a miracle. "I heard his voice! I actually heard!" A throng of eager spectators jammed around Bell's booth. Word flashed through the hall that Bell had created the greatest wonder of the mechanical world.

The telephone swept the exposition and the nation's imagination like a raging storm. Bell won the grand prize at the fair. Gray won a medal for his harmonic telegraph and reluctantly admitted that his telephone still could not transmit as clear a voice as did Bell's.

WHAT FOLLOWS A TRIUMPH?

There was still much work to be done on Bell's telephone. Bell's equipment could transmit voice only a few hundred yards. No thought had yet been given to how to create a network of phones or a switchboard system. These problems seemed trivial compared with the miracles already achieved.

In October of that same year, 1876, Bell and Watson held the first two-way conversation between Boston and Cambridge, a distance of 3 miles (5 km). By the end of the month, they had increased that to the "significant distance" of 137 miles (220 km). Further improvement that winter resulted in a second patent being issued in 1877. In this patent application, Bell uses the word "telephone" to describe his invention. Also in 1877 Hubbard, Sanders, Bell, and Watson formed the Bell Telephone Company.

Fame and fortune had arrived for Bell. The telephone freed Alexander Graham Bell. The decade from 1866 to 1876 had been one of intensive, stressful, and detailed work, study, and experimentation. Since 1864, he had worked in the shadow of his father and his father's Visible Speech system. With the telephone, Bell broke into the international limelight—on his own—with his own creation. He was now released from the confines of daily students and classes, freed to be an inventor instead of a teacher. He was no longer Professor Bell's son, carrying on the family work of Visible Speech. He was suddenly Alexander Graham Bell, internationally renowned inventor, the most famous Bell of all.

Bell's telephone was about to start a communication revolution.

In the flush of victory, Alexander married Mabel on July 11, 1877. The couple honeymooned in England while promoting the telephone. Because of his fame—and possibly because of his Scottish roots—Alexander was allowed to demonstrate his telephone for Queen Victoria. The queen was impressed. Bell's telephone was on the way to becoming an international mainstay of life.

Still the road to a working telephone system was far from smooth. Technical problems nagged the fledgling Bell Company for decades to come. More than six hundred lawsuits and legal fights challenged Bell's exclusive patent rights to create and sell telephones. Two suits even reached the Supreme Court. Bell (and his vast team of lawyers) won each and every fight. The last one dragged on until 1893.

The telephone was Bell's. The year was 1877. He was free to pursue his grandest imaginings and his every inventive whim. And Alexander Graham Bell was still only thirty years old.

NINE

The Fires of Invention

During the next few years, Bell was plagued by an endless flood of demands for technical improvements to his telephone system. To make the telephone practical, he had to increase the effective transmission distance between signal booster stations. Bell had created his original system with just two telephones and one wire connecting them. But if telephones were to serve various businesses and homes, he had to create a network of telephones. He also had to invent some kind of switching system.

He needed to find ways to improve sound quality so that what listeners heard sounded like the voice of the speaker. Wires were hurriedly strung like spiderwebs up and down streets, often fifty—even a hundred—lines running down a single street corridor, hanging from each pole's crossbars like spars on a ship's mast. But snow and wind often broke the wires or toppled the poles. Lightning and heavy rain disrupted transmissions. Suppliers didn't (or couldn't) meet the detailed specifications Bell demanded for the vast array of parts they provided.

There were seemingly endless legal challenges to his monopoly on the mushrooming telephone service—enough to fill the time of twenty lawyers. Worse, many of the suits attacked Bell's character. He was accused of perjury, of bribing government officials, of forgery, and of stealing the work of others, especially that of German inventor Philip Reis, who had developed a system for sending tones down an electric wire in 1860 and a multiple-channel version in 1875. In suit after suit,

The Growth of a Giant

The telephone was invented in 1876. By the next spring, the first switchboard appeared in Boston. The first phone directory was printed for New Haven, Connecticut, in 1878, with the first Yellow Pages appearing in 1886. By 1880, 47,900 phones were in use in the United States. Even though no one could talk beyond his or her local switchboard's reach—that is, outside of his or her own community or telephone "exchange."

The first pay phone appeared in New York in 1889. That same year, the first rotary-dial phone was built in Kansas City. Transcontinental links between switchboards did not exist until 1915. The last local operator switchboard in the United States was not replaced by direct-dial automatic switching until 1976.

The first Touch-Tone phone was sold in 1964; pagers arrived in the marketplace in 1974. The first cordless phone appeared around 1980.

not only Bell's invention but his very name and reputation were dragged through the mud.

Bell won every one of those suits.

Legal victory gave Bell no pleasure. His soul had been deeply wounded by the attacks. Alexander was an inventor. Legal questions and technicalities couldn't hold his attention for long. He took away from his decade-long pursuit of the telephone not a love of telephones but a love for the process of invention—the struggle to identify solutions, the thrill of creating them, the unequaled rush of success. Managing a company—even a giant empire like the Bell Telephone Company— could not compare.

Certainly, he appreciated his accomplishment, and he greatly enjoyed the financial stability of his achievement, but he craved the thrill of being totally immersed in the headlong rush to create. The period immediately following the creation of the telephone became one of the most creative and productive periods of Bell's life, a period that produced more inventions a year than did any other. From 1878 to 1882, new inventions spun out of Bell's mind and into working completion at a bewildering rate.

In the summer of 1877, Alexander and his bride, Mabel, sailed to England. The trip was intended as a short honeymoon, but Bell soon extended it. One reason, certainly, was to enjoy England and Scotland. A second was because of Mabel's pregnancy. But just as certainly, one reason was to hide from the technical and legal hounding surrounding the telephone. In early 1878 he told his wife, "I am sick to death of telephones!"

The Bells' first daughter, Elsie May, was born in London on May 8, 1878. In the fall, Bell traveled to Scotland, where he had been invited to open a school for the deaf. Bell taught there for several weeks before returning to London. During that period he wrote to Mabel, "I am immensely happy, the happiest I have been since that whole business [the telephone] began. I know I will always be known first as a teacher of the deaf."

That statement was doubly ironic. First, Bell would never again, during the remaining forty-four years of his life, teach in a classroom. Second, future generations would hear of his work with the deaf only as a footnote to his inventions—primarily that of the telephone.

THE RETURN OF INVENTION

The inventive spirit smoldered just under Alexander's teacher façade and would not be ignored. In late 1878, Alexander brought his wife and daughter back to Canada and was hard at work in his own Boston lab, beginning to design a machine that could measure hearing loss.

In spring of 1879, the Bells moved from Boston to Washington, D.C., for several reasons: to be closer to Mabel's

Mabel holds the new addition to the Bell family, Elsie May.

parents, to be available for the bulging number of lawsuits that were being tried in Washington courts, and to be closer to the Bell company offices and the work being done to develop a national telephone system.

In Bell's Washington lab, he adapted elements of his discarded design for a harmonic telegraph into a machine that could send a series of different tones to a small speaker held against a patient's ear. By recording how well that person heard each of the tones, Bell could create a profile of the person's hearing. He called the machine an audiometer.

His greatest stumbling block for the audiometer was that there existed no units of measure for sound volume, no way to measure exactly how much louder one sound was than another. How could he send precisely the same volume of each tone through his audiometer if there were no way to measure sound volume?

Bell decided to invent a unit of sound volume, and he did. That unit of measure was later named the "bel" in his honor. Sound is commonly measured in tenths of a bel, or in decibels (dB). Every amplifier, speaker, satellite dish, and radio transmission on Earth is measured and designed using decibels as the key units for calculating the intensity, or volume, of a sound.

The inventor's audiometer could now transmit each tone to a patient's speaker at progressively lower volumes. The listener then recorded whether or not he or she could hear the tones. The results created an exact profile of a person's hearing over the entire frequency range of human hearing.

The audiometer became an instant success with the medical community. It gave doctors a kind of diagnostic tool they had never had before. Modern hearing tests use the same principles and techniques Bell created for his original design.

Bell had now tried to invent three devices. Two were smash successes. The telephone revolutionized communications around the world. The audiometer revolutionized medical assessment of hearing loss and led to vastly improved treatment for partial deafness. Only his attempt to create a harmonic telegraph had failed. That failure could easily be brushed aside, however, since Bell's focus had swayed from telegraph to telephone.

As the 1880s began, Bell was feeling supremely confident in his technical abilities, just as the nation was feeling upbeat and confident about its future. But the legal attacks of the late 1870s had left a permanent scar on Bell. He had become reclusive. He refused most requests for interviews, fearing that his words would be misquoted or misused. He never gave autographs for fear that his signature would be moved to some other document and used against him in court. He wrote in a card to his wife, "I would be a hermit if not for you."

Though totally deaf, Mabel was able to converse using lipreading and the Visible Speech techniques Alexander had taught her. Still, her speech was slow and often difficult to understand. Yet it was Mabel who maintained a social life for the Bells and who pushed Alexander into Washington social circles.

In Washington, Bell worked with a young engineer, Charles Sumner Tainter, who had been trained at the same Charles Williams Electrical Supply Company in Boston where Bell met Thomas Watson. That winter Bell and Tainter picked up an old idea that Bell had dreamed of and set aside.

Bell dreamed of transmitting a voice signal not through clunky wires that needed regular booster amplifiers, that broke, and that were costly and unsightly, but through beams of light over a device Bell named a photophone. Bell was in the lab, working on his photophone, when his second daughter, Marian (called Daisy) was born in their Washington, D.C., home on February 15.

On February 19, 1880, Bell and Tainter were able to make the photophone work. The device was both elegant and simple. A narrow beam of light was aimed at a small, thin mirror. From the mirror, this light beam reflected into an opening in the photophone transmitter where it fell on a selenium element that could change light energy into electric current (as modern photocells do).

When a person talked into the photophone's mouthpiece, his or her voice was directed against the thin mirror that then vibrated with the airwaves of the voice. As the mirror vibrated, so too would the reflected beam of light, so that the intensity of the light beam reaching the selenium chip flickered and varied. In turn, this made the electrical current vary because the amount of electricity the selenium chip produced depended on the intensity of the light that struck it.

On the other end, the process could be reversed to produce soundwave vibrations at the receiver. Sound waves of human speech produced corresponding variations in the intensity of a light beam that produced exactly the same variations in an electric current.

Bell declared, "I have heard a ray of sun laugh, cough, and sing!"

Bell could make it work, but no one knew what to do with the thing. It didn't seem practical. In fact, Bell's photophone was simply too far ahead of its time. It was to be nearly eighty years before modern engineers would use fiber-optic cables to again transmit voice signals over beams of light. The photophone worked, but it was a commercial flop.

In the fall of 1880, Bell won the French Volta Prize (created by Napoleon in 1805 to reward scientific development). The prize came with a $10,000 award, which Bell used to open a bigger research facility, the Volta Laboratory, in Washington.

THE TRAGEDY OF DEATH

Undiscouraged, Bell charged into 1881. But in that year, tragedy was to both direct and diminish Bell's inventive spirit.

Mabel was pregnant with their third child when, on July 2, 1881, President James Garfield was shot by an assassin at a Washington, D.C., train station. The president lay ashen, weak, and near death with a bullet lodged deep in his body—a bullet doctors were unable to find. They asked Alexander Bell if he could do anything to locate the deadly slug.

Bell spent three frantic weeks designing an electric metal detector (the world's first metal detector)—one that worked much as modern

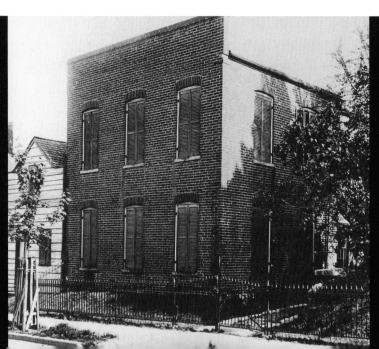

With the money Bell won, he built a new, larger laboratory. He named it the Volta Laboratory.

minesweepers and handheld metal detectors do today. He tested the device on thirty Civil War veterans who still carried bullets deep in their bodies and, in every case, was able to locate the metal slug. He took his detector and a revolver to a butcher's shop, fired several bullets into sides of beef, and easily found each with his detector.

Bell proudly marched to Garfield's bedside with his metal detector—and failed to locate the president's bullet on three attempts. Dumbfounded and unable to comprehend his failure, he was ushered out by aides.

Bell worked compulsively for another two weeks to develop a second design. This detector used a thin metal probe that had to be inserted in the patient's body but produced more accurate results than had his first design.

On August 1, Bell rushed back to Garfield's room with his new detector. Bell's new metal detector indicated that the bullet was lodged very deep in the president's body, near the spine. Based on this information, doctors operated and probed for the bullet but never found it.

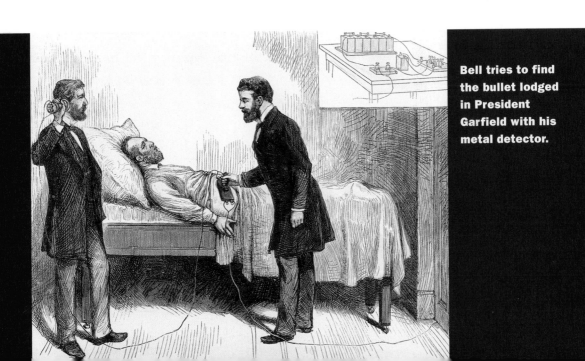

Bell tries to find the bullet lodged in President Garfield with his metal detector.

None of these doctors washed or sterilized their hands or probes. (Lister had discovered sterilization techniques in 1865, but his theories had not been widely adapted by 1880.) During one of these probes, a doctor's finger ruptured the president's liver. A small hole had been turned into a twenty-inch gash. Massive infection started in the now-gaping wound.

Only after the president had died on September 19—seventy-nine days after he was shot—did Bell realize why his first detector had failed. Garfield lay on a bed with metal springs. The metal springs overpowered the detector and concealed the small bullet. There had been nothing wrong with the detector at all!

Bell was not comforted by this revelation. The press and the scientific community tried to make him the villain for his failure to save the president's life. Doctors and hospitals, however, hailed Bell's second metal detector as a great advance for surgical medicine. The device was a staple in most operating rooms until replaced by X-ray machines almost twenty years later. Even this praise and the metal detector's moderate commercial success failed to comfort Bell.

In a somber mood he returned to Massachusetts (where Mabel had traveled to stay with relatives while he was working on his metal

Bell Blamed for Death

After President Garfield died, the Washington press turned not on the doctors but on Bell. He was called incompetent. The press accused Bell of having killed the president. Three senators called for hearings on how Bell had botched the case.

detector), only to be met with a second tragedy. Mabel gave birth to their third child, a boy, on August 15, 1881. Though a "strapping" big boy, Edward was unable to breathe properly on his own. Attending doctors didn't know what to do, and the boy died within hours of his birth. Mabel said—and wrote in letters—that she believed that the boy might have lived if only Alexander had been with her in the days before the baby was born instead of in Washington.

Bell was devastated and wracked with guilt. He felt as if a giant weight had fallen on his shoulders and crushed the spark out of him. In mourning, he shut himself in his lab, where intense work became his therapy as he feverishly designed and built what he called a vacuum jacket.

The first one he made was small, as if designed for a baby, as if he hoped somehow to rescue his own lost son. Others were larger. The jacket fit tightly over a patient's upper body. A hand-pumped bellows pumped air in and out and was attached to air pockets in the jacket. When the bellows sucked air out, emptying the pockets, it created a vacuum that would force the patient's chest to expand and breathe. When the bellows blew air into the pockets, it created a positive pressure that forcibly collapsed the patient's lungs into an exhale. The jacket literally forced the wearer's lungs to breathe in and out even when the patient's own muscles and nerves had failed.

It was simple. It was effective. It was too late to save Alexander's son. Bell's vacuum jacket was the forerunner of the iron lung—a metal breathing cylinder that patients lay in up to their neck—that was invented fifty years later to aid victims of polio in breathing. The vacuum jacket was heralded by doctors but found scant commercial success.

Bell worked with Charles Sumner Tainter, who was the driving force behind the invention of the graphophone.

During 1882, Bell returned to Washington to work intermittently at the Volta lab with Tainter. But there was no drive, no spark in Bell's efforts. Tainter took the lead, working mostly with other engineers in designing the last great invention of this period of Bell's life: the graphophone, a device able to record a person's voice.

Bell's graphophone significantly improved on the original Edison phonograph created in December of 1877, and evolved into the Dictaphone and the creation of the Dictaphone Company.

Bell had created a flurry of remarkable inventions during this short period. None could touch the fame or financial success of the telephone. Still, all were valuable, successful, and important. He had truly established himself as a major inventor.

TEN

Ahead of His Time

Naturally reserved and aloof, Alexander Bell turned inward. He now clung close to his family and shied away from society, invention, and work. For several years after the dual tragedies of 1881, he did little more than dabble aimlessly at various ideas. The death of his son dredged up the bitter and terrifying memories of losing Ted and Melly. The failure of his invention to save President Garfield's life weighed on his conscience. When required to, he helped with lawsuits and Bell Telephone Company technical matters. But he showed little creative drive.

Bell could not thrive in the Washington, D.C., world of social and political intrigue, pressure, and maneuvering. It stifled and suffocated him. The lawsuits dragged on. Bell company engineers hounded him to work on the phone system. He needed to get away.

In 1885, after some very difficult times, the Bell family decided to go on vacation. From left to right, this photograph shows Elsie, Mabel, Marian, and Alexander Bell around the time of their trip.

In 1885 Bell packed his family onto a ship for an extended vacation in Canada. In rough seas the ship hit rocks and foundered off the coast of Newfoundland. It was officially listed as a shipwreck. Alexander called it a "rough landing."

The family traveled on to Nova Scotia and settled in the small town of Baddeck on Cape Breton Island. Instantly the town, with its long, twisting harbor on the north arm of a sinewy lake and open, rolling hills, tugged at Bell's heart. The hills looked, smelled, and felt like Scotland. The weather reminded Bell of Scotland. Baddeck felt like home. It also felt like a blessed sanctuary far from the chaos and endless demands of Washington.

During the next seven years, Bell bought an entire peninsula just across the bay from Baddeck. He named it Beinn Bhreagh (pronounced *ben vree-ah*)—"Beautiful Mountain" in Gaelic.

Baddeck was a small, isolated town with few amenities or services. Bell had to improvise to supply his family with the comforts of a leisurely country life. From an automatic butter churner to a water delivery system to cooling fans to electricity production—the inventive necessities of rural country living occupied Bell's drive for invention. Beinn Bhreagh also accommodated his desire for isolation. For the first two years that Bell lived on his peninsula, he had no telephone.

But an inventor's mind is a restless and ruthless master. By mid-1887 Bell found his mind first musing about, and then obsessively craving, new discoveries. But his imagination would not latch onto one specific idea (like a telephone), or even onto one general subject area (like electrical communications) as it had in past years. Instead, Bell simultaneously shot out in four very distinct directions: flight, genetics, hydrofoil boats, and resource conservation.

By 1890 Alexander was conducting experiments in all four areas and continued to do so (whether he produced any tangible results or not) until his death in 1922. In each of these areas Bell's ideas leaped

Today, Beinn Bhreagh is the Alexander Graham Bell National Historic Site of Canada. Visitors can learn about Bell's life by touring exhibits, watching films on Bell, and attending programs given by the site's staff.

decades ahead of his time. He had the vision, but lacked the necessary mathematical and scientific knowledge to translate his ideas into reality. The telephone was the perfect invention for its time. It met a recognized, crucial need. Bell's ideas in these new areas were too far ahead of their time to be recognized or valued.

Over these last thirty years or so of his life, Bell bounced from one idea to another without doing the necessary in-depth background research to fully understand any of the individual scientific fields. Alexander also spent considerable time and money supporting the work of other scientists and the creation of several important science-related publications.

TAKING FLIGHT

Alexander Bell began formal experiments in aviation in 1891. By the time of his death, he had conducted more than 1,200 aviation experiments! But his thinking on the topic dates back nearly fifteen years before he began his experiments. In 1878 Bell drew sketches of a motorized flying machine complete with ailerons (movable flaps at the tips of airplane wings). Those sketches predated the Wright brothers' first flight by twenty-five years. They predate the adoption of ailerons into active airplane designs by thirty years! By 1878, however, Bell was married and overwhelmed by telephone affairs. He had no time to pursue his dream of a flying machine.

In 1893, Bell sketched a design for a jet airplane—fifty years before the first jet engines were tested in Germany. In that same year, and after only tinkering with kites and gliders, Bell pronounced that the "problems of aerial navigation will be solved within a decade and will revolutionize travel."

Exactly one decade later, the Wright brothers flew.

Long before the Wright brothers flew, however, Bell was deep into his own aviation experiments—determining how much thrust (power) could be achieved with different shapes and numbers of propellers, with different angles of the propeller blade, and with different types of engines. Most of Bell's experiments used steam-powered engines.

Samuel Langley, secretary of the Smithsonian Institution, published a paper in 1891 describing his general design for a motorized aerodrome (flying machine). Bell was enchanted by Langley's ideas, and in 1894, Bell agreed both to finance and to physically help Langley's work if he would conduct his test flights at Beinn Bhreagh. Langley would continue to conduct his basic research in Washington, D.C. In 1896, Langley's and Bell's 14-foot (4.25-meter) span, steam-powered model aerodrome

Manned Flight

Bell used the term *aerodrome* (from the Greek words meaning "crossing the air") for his planes as early as 1878. The Wright brothers, Wilbur and Orville, called theirs an *aeroplane*. Bell scoffed that "plane" referred only to the wing surface that provided lift. Still *aeroplane* caught on and, by 1918, had been simplified to *airplane* in the United States.

The Wright brothers' plane weighed 605 pounds (274.4 kilograms)— 750 pounds (340.2 kg) fully loaded. The plane flew for twelve seconds on its first flight on December 17, 1903. The Wrights had not taken more fuel for a longer flight, because they feared it would add too much weight.

flew more than 3,000 feet (914.4 m) before it lost steam and gently glided back to Earth. Bell wrote that "without a doubt, the practicality of heavier than air flight has been demonstrated."

They planned to scale up to a plane capable of carrying a human passenger. However, later that year, German aviator Otto Lilienthal died when his experimental glider crashed. The death shocked Bell. He became cautious, afraid to risk his or another's life by taking the next necessary step in his experiments: manned aerodrome flights. His mind turned to other ideas and did not return to fixed-wing powered flight until 1907.

One of these other ideas was tetrahedral cells—four-sided objects where each side is a triangle. A pyramid having a triangular base is an example of a tetrahedral cell. Bell realized that frames made of tetrahedral cells would be lightweight and exceptionally strong. Long rows of tetrahedrons could be joined together to fashion giant towers—or wings. Bell began a long series of experiments with giant tetrahedral kites that culminated in 1906 when one of his kites lifted two men off the ground.

As always, each success drove Bell into his Mohawk war dance and delirious whoops of joy. After he photographed a man flying with his tetrahedral kite, Mabel wrote, "Each triumph means so terribly much to him. Each time it is as if he has lived only for this one day."

Bell (far right) observes as one of his tetrahedral kites is readied for an experiment.

By 1906, the world "knew" that the Wright brothers had flown. However, few people had been allowed to see their plane or to see them fly, since they were afraid of being copied until they had sold their design to the government. Bell, fast approaching his sixtieth birthday, longed to make his mark in the world of flight. His mind returned to powered flight.

In 1907 he formed the Aerial Experiment Association (AEA) to "successfully demonstrate manned motorized flight" using Mabel's money to back the venture. Bell's AEA is credited with many of the airplane advances of the following two years. The association drew aviation pioneers from across the country to Bell's peninsula to work on new designs. The initial test flight of AEA's first plane called *Red Wing* took place in 1907. It was the first-ever publicly viewed flight of a heavier-than-air flying machine. AEA's second plane, *White Wing*, flew to standing ovations through much of 1908. *White Wing* was the first aeroplane to incorporate two key Bell innovations: a three-wheel undercarriage for landings and takeoffs, and hinged movable flaps on the back side of each wing, called ailerons, for stability and maneuvering control.

AEA's next plane, *June Bug*, flew more than 150 flights without a single problem (a record) and won the *Scientific American* trophy for being the first airplane to fly more than a kilometer in public demonstration. It actually flew over 5,000 feet (1,524 m). The AEA's final design, *Silver Dart*, set ten speed, endurance, and altitude records during January and February 1909.

The AEA had accomplished its goal and disbanded in March of 1909. Bell's team of engineers had become the most advanced airplane designers and builders in the world. Bell planned to form a company to continue their work, but he gave it insufficient time and attention, having already turned his primary focus to hydrofoil boats. If he had allowed flight to be his sole focus, it is possible that we would associate his name with the greatest developments in early aviation.

SEARCHING FOR GENES

The second field that caught Bell's fancy was heredity. In the late 1880s, the study of heredity was a new science, having been created by Austrian Gregor Mendel in the late 1860s. Mendel determined that each parent passes a bundle of traits (genes) to his or her offspring. Around 1890, Bell began to wonder if deafness was a trait that could be inherited.

There was no way for Bell to experiment with human deafness. In 1889 he turned to sheep breeding to investigate how traits are passed through generations in sheep. Bell hired a sheep breeder to manage his growing flock and began thirty years of breeding experiments. One of his sheep strains was noted for exceptionally thick and luxurious wool, but the attempt to breed sheep with more nipples to encourage the birth of twins failed in its purpose and produced sheep with thin, mangy

This photograph of *June Bug* was taken in Hammondsport, New York.

Gregor Mendel's Peas

Austrian monk Gregor Mendel experimented with varieties of peas. Generation after generation, he carefully cross-pollinated his parent plants and watched for their characteristics, such as tall or short, yellow or green, to appear in the next generations. He found that a consistent pattern of dominant and passive traits were passed on by each parent plant. From his work—first published in 1865 and then translated and "rediscovered" in the mid-1880s—the entire science of genetics arose.

wool. Bell achieved neither major innovations nor breakthroughs in the science of genetics.

By 1910, Bell's interest in genetics turned to a study of longevity. Why did some people live longer than others? Was it something about the way in which they lived their lives, or was longevity inherited through the family genes? As with so many of his other later studies, Bell lacked sufficient technical knowledge of the particular scientific field to conduct serious work beyond his usual intense pondering and visioning. He finally concluded that no, longevity was not passed on but that the ability to fight disease was, and that contributed to longevity. But he produced neither hard data nor studies to back up this conclusion.

Another area in which Bell pioneered without much commercial success was resource conservation and recycling. In the early 1890s he envisioned the first of a series of schemes for recycling water and focused for several years on recapturing the exhaled water vapor in every breath. Bell's device worked, but it was impractical for everyday use and never produced enough water to make it worthwhile. By 1900 he had shifted to other condensation schemes as well as to the conversion of saltwater into fresh and a number of other designs and ideas, but he achieved no significant results.

During this period, Bell designed one of the world's first electric heaters in order to reduce the deadly pollution of excessive coal burning. He also experimented with heat recycling plans, and built several crude solar heaters. Again, these devices worked but drew little public interest and found no commercial success.

Less than fifty years after his death, in the throes of our worldwide "energy crisis," Bell's ideas were finally appreciated. His designs, updated by improved materials and engineering concepts, flourished beginning in the 1960s. Bell's lasting legacy in the area of conservation came not through his mechanical inventions but through a term he invented. It was a term that didn't catch on in 1914 when he first used it but is known to almost everyone today.

The term is *greenhouse effect*. Bell used it first in a general way to describe the effect of atmosphere pollution. Through the work of others, the term now describes more specifically the effect that burning fossil fuels have on the atmosphere and on long-term weather patterns. It was also Alexander Graham Bell who first predicted the energy crisis that began in the 1970s and the severe resource shortages that currently plague our planet. Yet in the dawn of the twentieth century, a skeptical world scoffed and dismissed his warnings as being unimaginably ridiculous.

HYDROFOILS AND RECORD NEEDLES

Bell's experimental fancy led him in several other directions during the last twenty years of his life. Chief among these was hydrofoil boat design. Bell's work with the design of airplane wings, combined with his lakeside location, created an opportunity for him to ponder better hull—the body and framework of a ship—designs. He began to wonder if he could use the principles of airplane wing lift to make a boat ride higher and more efficiently in the water.

Hydrofoils are underwater wings that lift a ship higher in the water, just as airplane wings lift a plane into the air, and thus allow ships to literally fly through water.

Bell began his experiments in 1906, studying pontoon boat designs. Bell's engineering assistant, Casey Baldwin, deserves much of the credit for their remarkable hydrofoil success. In 1908, Bell and Baldwin began to build and test model hydrofoils. They built the first full-scale hydrofoil model in 1911: the HD-1. Bell loved to watch from shore as his HD-1 skimmed happily across Baddeck Bay at the unheard-of speed of 35 miles per hour (mph), a boat speed record at the time.

By 1919, Bell had graduated to his monstrous, 60-foot (18-m) hydrofoil, the HD-4. Powered by twin 350-horsepower Liberty engines (on loan from the U.S. Navy), the HD-4 roared loudly enough to frighten spectators 0.25 mile (0.4 km) away. At 15 mph, the HD-4 began to rise higher in the water. At 30 mph the underwater wings produced so much lift that the boat rose completely out of the water, water streaming from its exposed hull. Only the winglike front and back hydrofoils and struts (metal poles connecting the hydrofoil wings to the boat's hull) remained submerged. At its top speed of 71 mph, the HD-4 was a thundering blur whose roar and speed made watchers tremble in awe and wonder. The HD-4 set a speed record that lasted for more than a decade.

Bell's musings during his last thirty years led him into experiments and studies in many separate areas—some absurd and some valuable. Alexander was one of the first to call for the use of radioactive radium implants to fight tumors. He also invented (through his Volta lab in Washington) in 1890 the stylus for phonograph records as well as the flat record. (Previously, all recordings had been made on cylinders.) Bell's share of the sale of the stylus patent rights netted $200,000.

Bell introduced the first X-ray machine into Canada in 1896—less than a year after its discovery in Germany. Bell also wrote a paper in 1908 in which he tried to show that gravity was a myth. It took the combined efforts of four friends in the scientific world to keep Bell from releasing the paper. He also continued to invent devices around the house to make life easier, such as a series of rope pulleys he fashioned in 1907 that allowed him to raise or lower any window in the house without leaving his porch swing lounge.

In 1902 Bell invented what he hoped would be a thought-transfer machine. Bell reasoned that if the brain worked by electromagnetic waves and impulses, he should be able to pick up those electrical impulses through an induction coil and transmit them down a wire to a receiver mounted on someone else's head. The best that Bell's thought-transfer machine could do was to give both people headaches at the same time (which Bell called encouraging).

What is remarkable in many of these areas is Bell's foresight, his vision. His ideas were decades ahead of his contemporaries'. What is most remarkable is that his foresight spread across such a wide variety of areas and fields. It is clear that Alexander Graham Bell could have made major contributions in virtually any of these areas if he had been able to focus his time and effort upon that one area. But that, of course, would have meant abandoning the others, something Alexander's driving curiosity would not allow him to do.

ELEVEN

Supporting the World

The telephone ensured financial luxury for Alexander Graham Bell. He used that wealth to finance the wide range of his own projects and experiments described in the previous chapter. In addition, Bell generously used his money to support the work of other scientists, to support efforts to publicize the progress made by science, and to support education (especially for the deaf).

While Bell's Volta Laboratory in Washington, D.C., concentrated on Bell's projects, it was, in part, designed to funnel support to the scientists Bell hired. The lab hired scientists and gave them wide freedom to develop their own projects and scientific areas of interest.

Bell gave funding to Albert Michelson, the American physicist struggling to accurately measure the speed of light. With Bell's support, Michelson succeeded and became the first American to win, in 1907, a scientific Nobel Prize.

Bell generously supported the work of Samuel Langley in the development of his steam-powered aerodrome, and he created the Aerial Experiment Association, which hired other scientists working in the area of manned, heavier-than-air flight, and funded their research. In total, Alexander Bell financed the work and development of more than twenty other scientists.

TELLING THE WORLD

Bell had always been vitally interested in educating the public about scientific advances and promoting those advances through publications. He started his first magazine, the short-lived *The Visible Speech Pioneer*, three years before he completed his working telephone. In all, Bell supported six publications to publicize science. Three have endured and are worth noting.

In 1882 Bell took over control of *Science* magazine, a periodical still published and regarded as a premier showcase for scientific discoveries. In 1888, Bell helped to create the National Geographic Society to make the world of natural sciences accessible to humankind. The monthly magazine of this society remains among the most successful and popular magazines ever created.

After working with Langley on aerodrome designs, Bell decided to financially support the fledgling Smithsonian Institution in Washington, D.C., and, in particular, its astrophysics observatory. He provided money to start its monthly magazine, which is still published and highly regarded.

In addition, in 1887, Bell created the Volta Bureau with the $200,000 he received from the sale of the patent rights for the phonograph stylus.

The Volta Bureau, which survived for thirty years, was charged with publicizing and promoting to the public education for the deaf.

Successfully creating any one of these endeavors would be impressive. Having started them all—while still maintaining a full schedule of his own experiments and projects—is astounding and attests to the energy, passion, intelligence, and drive that characterized Alexander Graham Bell's life.

The National Geographic Society was established in 1888. Bell's father-in-law was its first president. American explorer Robert Peary (with the moustache and cane) and Alexander Graham Bell (third from Peary's left) were a few of its distinguished members.

American Magazines

One of the first American magazines, *Memoirs of the American Academy of Arts and Sciences*, was first published in 1783. Popular local magazines began to appear by 1803. Because of slow, expensive, and spotty postal service, national magazines did not appear until the late 1840s. *Harper's Magazine*, which appeared in 1850, and *Vanity Fair* magazine, which appeared in 1860, were two of the first magazines successful with a national readership. The chief competition of magazines were the sensationalized "penny papers," daily papers that read like modern tabloids.

Magazines flourished during the Civil War, when there was an insatiable demand for accounts from the front. The number of American magazines tripled during that four-year period. Readership increased tenfold.

Several science magazines, including *Popular Science Monthly*, existed by the time Bell began his support and control of *Science* and *National Geographic* magazines.

The Bell family and guests celebrate the ground-breaking of the Volta Bureau in Washington, D.C. Attendees included Elsie May Bell, Annie Sullivan, Helen Keller, and Marian "Daisy" Bell (seated on the ground, left to right). Eliza Bell (seated in chair, right) and Mabel Bell (standing next to Eliza, holding piece of paper) were also present. Alexander Graham Bell is in the back row behind Mabel.

BELL'S FIRST LOVE

In Alexander's mind, he was first and foremost an educator of the deaf. He founded schools for the deaf in Scotland and Washington, D.C., and worked closely with schools in Boston and Nova Scotia. But he did far more than start private schools. Most of the publications he founded were designed to enlighten the public about science and education. He founded the Volta Bureau and, in 1890, the American Association for the Teaching of Speech to the Deaf. It was later renamed The A. G. Bell Association for the Deaf.

When Bell heard of Helen Keller, a deaf and blind girl, he assisted in finding a teacher willing to train her and helped pay for Helen's education. In 1911 Bell financed the educational research and work of Maria Montessori—founder of the popular and successful Montessori schools.

Bell's one disappointment in the realm of education was his ongoing battle with Edward Gallaudet over deaf education. The dispute focused on their differing theories and approaches to teaching the deaf how to communicate. Bell wanted to teach the deaf to talk using Visible Speech and other verbal techniques. Gallaudet preferred teaching the deaf to use sign language so that they could "hear" with their eyes.

Bell argued that, since the general public didn't know sign language, Gallaudet's system would block communication between the deaf and the speaking world. Gallaudet countered that, if the deaf spoke, they wouldn't be able to hear or understand the reply.

Neither side would consider compromise, and neither side would acknowledge value in the opposing approach. Neither man would relent. Eventually, Gallaudet's sign language gained popular favor. Bell's Visible Speech was abandoned. Today virtually every hearing-impaired person learns sign language. It was a bitter defeat for Alexander Graham Bell, who had dedicated so much of his life both to deaf education and to Visible Speech.

By 1900, Bell also became an active supporter of the women's suffrage movement. He helped fund and support a 1913 suffrage march in Washington, D.C. He remained a firm and active supporter of women's rights until his death in 1922.

It would have been easy for Alexander Graham Bell to be absorbed by his own work, to focus on his own importance, but he never allowed himself that arrogance. Throughout the last thirty years of his life, he was as concerned with the scientific work of others, with education, and with scientific journals as with his own research efforts. Making a significant contribution in any one of these areas would have been a great and noteworthy undertaking. That Bell made major contributions in them all is astonishing. Even more remarkable is that Bell is remembered for none of these aspects of his life and work. Each of these noteworthy accomplishments and contributions has been overshadowed by his one extraordinary invention—the telephone.

TWELVE

The Life of a Visionary

Alexander Graham Bell invented the telephone and is famous for that invention. But the telephone did more for Bell than Bell did for the telephone. If Bell hadn't invented it, either Gray or Edison would have created a working telephone system before the end of 1876. The communications development of the United States would not have been much affected.

But the telephone completely changed Alexander's life—all because he won the race and produced the first working telephone. Alexander's financial rewards from the telephone gave him the freedom to pursue whatever work struck a chord of interest in a wide variety of areas—work that was often original and revolutionary in its vision.

Alexander Graham Bell was an inventor, a tinkerer, a visionary, an educator, and a driven and compulsive worker. Was he the scientist he

Alexander Graham Bell approached his work with great dedication.

always wanted to be? Most would answer "no." His work was too scattered and unfocused. He never spent enough time in any one field to gain the expertise necessary to advance that topic. He did not keep up on developments and other research. He never gained mastery of mathematics, the prime language of science.

Bell was fortunate. He lived at the end of a period of scientific development when it was possible for an individual to make significant discoveries without being part a large, multidisciplinary team, a period when discovery in science did not require the vast funding of institutions that it does today. In a sense, he was one of the last great "amateur" scientist-inventors.

Bell threw himself headlong into every project with great energy, passion, tremendous intuitive insight, vision, and abundant drive and tenacity. Those qualities gave him a rich and rewarding life filled with triumphs. He found great joy from his experiments and from the process of engineering and scientific investigation. He was a doting father and grandfather and a loving husband to Mabel.

Certainly, Bell suffered through his share of sorrows. He was deeply saddened by the loss of both of his brothers and the death of his son. Professionally, he was disappointed in his inventive failures, his nagging lack of credibility in the scientific community, the preference of sign language to Visible Speech by the deaf community in the United States, and the degradation of hounding lawsuits.

On balance, Bell's joys and triumphs outweighed his sorrows. He achieved one phenomenal commercial success, the telephone, but he produced a wide variety of other valuable inventive successes: the phonograph stylus, flat records, the metal detector, audiometer, Dictaphone, tetrahedral cell construction, *Science*, the *Smithsonian*, and *National Geographic* magazines, and advanced hydrofoil design. Many of these would have individually made his life noteworthy on their own merit had they not been totally overshadowed by the telephone.

Alexander Graham Bell was a true science visionary in an amazingly wide variety of areas: resource conservation and aviation. None of his work in these areas came to completion during his lifetime.

Measured from the viewpoint of the rest of the world, the life of Alexander Graham Bell was a resounding success. The value of his many gifts of invention to the world is almost incalculable.

His own assessment would be more complex. His inventive successes meant less to him than the excitement of the next experiment, the next creation. His failures wounded him deeply. He lived a life that made our world a better place. He died at the age of seventy-five in his beloved Nova Scotia home on August 2, 1922. During his funeral on

August 4, every telephone in North America (more than 10 million of them) went silent for one minute. That final silence was a fitting tribute to a man who had dedicated his life to helping the deaf.

Alexander Graham Bell enjoys the natural surroundings of his beloved Beinn Bhreagh with his wife, Mabel, during his later years. The world lost a great inventive mind when he died on August 2, 1922.

Timeline

1876 Bell receives the first patent for a telephone on March 7. Bell finally transmits his first words on March 10. Bell demonstrates his telephone at the Centennial Exposition in Philadelphia and wins the Grand Prize in June.

1877 Bell marries Mabel Hubbard on July 11.

1878 Daughter Elsie is born in London on May 8.

1879 Bell invents the audiometer and the bel unit to measure loudness.

Thomas Edison invents the electric light.

1880 Bell creates the Volta Laboratory in Washington, D.C. Daughter Marian (Daisy) is born in Washington, on February 15.

1881 Bell's son, Edward, is born and dies from lung failure hours later. Bell invents the vacuum jacket respirator and the metal detector.

President Garfield is killed by an assassin.

1886 Bell moves to Nova Scotia and buys land for Beinn Bhreagh.

1889 Bell begins first of 1,200 experiments in aviation and starts research on sheep heredity.

1890 Bell invents flat record and stylus needle.

1903 Orville Wright makes the first powered flight on December 17.

1907 Bell forms the Aerial Experiment Association to demonstrate manned flight.

1909 AEA disbands in March after stirring success with *Red Wing, White Wing, June Bug,* and *Silver Dart.*

1911 Bell builds HD-1, his first hydrofoil boat.

1914 World War I begins.

1918 World War I ends on November 11.

1919 Bell builds HD-4, a 71-mph, record-setting hydrofoil.

1922 Bell dies at Beinn Bhreagh in Nova Scotia on August 2.

To Find Out More

BOOKS

Fisher, Leonard. *Alexander Graham Bell*. New York: Atheneum Books for Young Readers, 1999.

Gains, Ann. *Alexander Graham Bell*. Vero Beach, FL: Rourke Books, 2002.

Ganeri, Anita. *Alexander Graham Bell*. London: Thameside Press, 2000.

Grosvenor, Edwin, and Morgan Wesson. *Alexander Graham Bell: The Life and Times of the Man Who Invented the Telephone*. New York: Harry N. Abrams, Inc., 1997.

MacLeod, Elizabeth. *Alexander Graham Bell: An Inventive Life*. Minneapolis: Kids Can Press, 1999.

Mathews, Tom. *Always Inventing: A Photobiography of Alexander Graham Bell*. Washington, D.C.: National Geographic Society, 1999.

Pasachoff, Naomi. *Alexander Graham Bell: Making Connections*. New York: Oxford University Press, 1996.

Schuman, Michael. *Alexander Graham Bell: Inventor and Teacher*. Springfield, NJ: Enslow Books, 1999.

ORGANIZATIONS AND ONLINE SITES

Alec Bell
http://www.alecbell.org/

Biographer Edwin Grosvenor's site highlights the data he collected for his book on Bell.

Alexander Graham Bell
http://www.alexandergrahambell.org

This site provides historical manuscripts, letters, a life summary, and extensive links to other sites.

Alexander Graham Bell: The Man
http://www.fitzgeraldstudio.com/html/bell/theman.html

This site contains a good summary of the Canadian portion of Bell's life and work.

The Alexander Graham Bell Association for the Deaf and Hard of Hearing
17 Volta Place NW
Washington, DC 20007
http://www.agbell.org/

This organization offers many programs to help deaf and hard-of-hearing children.

The Alexander Graham Bell Institute
http://bell.uccb.ns.ca

This organization is dedicated to preserving Bell's legacy and making his papers more easily accessible. It also sponsors research.

Library of Congress
http://www.loc.gov/spcoll/026.html

This section of the Library of Congress provides information on Bell's life.

Library of Congress's American Treasures
http://www.loc.gov/exhibits/treasures/trr002.html

This part of the Library of Congress site allows visitors to view a collection of historical documents about and by Bell.

The Telephone History Website
http://atcaonline.com/phone/bell.htm

This site provides interesting details on Bell's inventive work.

A Note on Sources

I prefer to read and compare many resources for a research-based project such as this biography. I read more than 230 sources during my research for this book. They included published books and articles as well as many of Bell's and Watson's personal writings.

I also tried to interview the author of each of the sources I used most heavily. Talking to the authors helps me understand what they included and excluded from their writing and research, their primary goal and purpose, and their focus in organizing their work. It also gives me a chance to find out which sources they relied on most heavily and why. In the course of researching this book I interviewed eleven other authors who have written about Alexander Graham Bell.

Since I was unable to interview Bell himself (he died in 1922), I read as many of his journals, notebooks, and speeches as I could. His personal writing gave me an insight into his thinking and attitudes, his hopes and struggles, his personality, and his personal vision, that I could not gain from other sources. I backed up this reading with phone interviews with four of Bell's living relatives. None of these people actually knew him, but through them I gained a sense of their family stories and the family image of the man Bell was.

As I read and research a subject, I look for agreements and disagreement between major sources. It never happens that every biographer and researcher will agree, that they will interpret the evidence the same way, that they will include the same events and evidence. Once I have identified the points of difference, I search for the greatest preponderance of evidence in original work to support one side or the other in that disagreement. This is partly accomplished through my interviews of other authors. I search for the most reasonable way to mesh these discrepancies into a most-probable version of what really happened. This, then, is the history I present in my own book.

Certainly, I recommend the books listed in the To Find Out More section. These are valuable and reliable accounts of Bell's life and I used each of them. I read books not specifically about Bell in order to link Bell's work to other events in the frantic world of invention and discovery during Bell's lifetime. Finally, I have found great value in some older sources, written closer to the actual events I described. Some of these additional sources that I found to be particularly useful include Robert V. Bell Bruce's *Alexander Graham Bell and the Conquest of Solitude,* Roger Burlingame's *Out of Silence into Sound: The Life of Alexander Graham Bell,* Thomas Costain's *The Chord of Steel: The Story of the Invention of the Telephone,* and Dorothy Eber's *Genius at Work: Images of Alexander Graham Bell.*

—*Kendall Haven*

Index

About the Author

The only West Point graduate to become a professional storyteller, Kendall Haven holds a doctorate in oceanography, and is a nationally recognized expert on the architecture and structure of stories.

He has performed for more than 3 million people in forty states and has published five audio tapes. Among his eighteen published books are eight collections of original, historically accurate stories including more than three hundred stories; two children's fiction books; and two instructional books on the use of story: *Write Right!*, on teaching creative writing, and *No-Sweat Storytelling*, on doing, using, and teaching storytelling.

Haven has been awarded the 2000, 1999, 1997, 1996, and 1995 Storytelling World Silver Awards for best story anthology, the 1993 International Festival Association Silver Award for best educational program at a major national festival, and the 1993 Corporation for Public Broadcasting Silver Award for best children's public radio production. He has twice been designated an American Library Association "Notable Recording Artist."

Haven teaches graduate-level classes on storytelling and on story writing for eight university systems and has performed at more than 3,500 schools from elementary through college at 200 major conferences and festivals, and has conducted faculty in-service workshops for more than 20,000 teachers and writing workshops for more than 60,000 students.